SO-BIL-211

FORD
TRACTORS

Text by Robert N. Pripps
Photography by Andrew Morland

Motorbooks International
Publishers & Wholesalers ®

*To Janice, the wife of my youth and
my faithful companion these
thirty-six years*

First published in 1990 by Motorbooks International Publishers & Wholesalers, P O Box 2, 729 Prospect Avenue, Osceola, WI 54020 USA

© Robert N. Pripps, text; Andrew Morland, photographs

All rights reserved. With the exception of quoting brief passages for the purposes of review no part of this publication may be reproduced without prior written permission from the publisher

Motorbooks International is a certified trademark, registered with the United States Patent Office

The information in this book is true and complete to the best of our knowledge. All recommendations are made without any guarantee on the part of the author or publisher, who also disclaim any liability incurred in connection with the use of this data or specific details

We recognize that some words, model names and designations, for example, mentioned herein are the property of the trademark holder. We use them for identification purposes only. This is not an official publication

Motorbooks International books are also available at discounts in bulk quantity for industrial or sales-promotional use. For details write to Special Sales Manager at the Publisher's address

Library of Congress Cataloging-in-Publication Data
Pripps, Robert N.
   Ford tractors / Robert N. Pripps, Andrew Morland.
     p. cm.
   ISBN 0-87938-471-9
   1. Ford tractors—History. I. Morland, Andrew. II Title.
TL233.5.P75 1990   90-35075
631.3'72—dc20   CIP

Printed and bound in Hong Kong

On the front cover: *The 1952 Ford 8N with a rare Funk Brothers V-8 conversion owned by Palmer Fossum of Northfield, Minnesota. The conversion kit placed an 8BA, 100 horsepower 1952 Ford V-8 in the tractor along with gearbox adaptors and adaptors for the front wheel attachment.*

On the back cover: *The red and gray color scheme of this 1955 Ford Model 501 Offset Workmaster from the Fossum Collection is unique among Ford tractors and is striking against the afternoon Minnesota sky.*

On the frontispiece: *A British-built Fordson, owned by Keith Dorey of Wareham, Dorset, England.*

On the title page: *This beautifully restored 1946 Ford-Ferguson Model 2N, owned by Leroy Folkerts of Forreston, Illinois, was featured in a February 1988 article in Gas Engines magazine. The art deco styling of the tractor came from the same Ford designers that penned the cars and trucks of the era.*

On the contents page: *Homer Clark of LaValle, Wisconsin, owns this 1940 Model 9N. Ford Tractor, Ferguson System—that Ford got top billing was never completely satisfactory to Ferguson. This underlying battle of egos may have portended the troubles ahead. Nevertheless, as long as Old Henry was at the helm of the Ford Motor Company, the gentleman's Handshake Agreement that fostered the N Series tractors worked.*

Contents

Preface

The name Ford Tractor immediately conjures a vision of the little gray tractor that can be seen at golf courses, at airports and at small farms across the United States. Although the Ford name has been on a variety of tractors—from the simplest garden type to four-wheel-drive monsters—over the last seventy years, only those made between 1939 and 1952 were the true Ford Tractors; tractors made before and after those years must be identified in some other way besides the name Ford Tractor.

Three models were true Ford Tractors: the 9N, made from 1939 to 1942; the 2N, made from 1942 to 1947; and the 8N, made from 1947 to 1952. Although the 9N and 2N were basically the same, the 8N was a considerable refinement. Nevertheless, all three continue to be lumped together under the heading of Ford Tractor.

Ford Tractors seem to be everywhere, but fewer than one million were built for worldwide distribution. When introduced over fifty years ago, they revolutionized the tractor industry. This is the story of these little gray tractors, of their heritage and of the human genius that engendered them. It is also the story of their descendents, and of the Ford Tractor as it is today.

Acknowledgments

Without the specific help of certain people, this book would not have been completed. Therefore, I would like to gratefully acknowledge their contributions:

Keith Oltrogge, publisher of the bimonthly newsletter *Wild Harvest, Massey Collectors News,* for information about the Ferguson tractors.

Gerard Rinaldi, publisher of *The 9N-2N-8N Newsletter,* for using his computer to locate photographic subjects in my vicinity.

Palmer Fossum, Ford Tractor collector, restorer and parts dealer from Northfield, Minnesota, who is a storehouse of tractor lore and a genuinely pleasant fellow to be around.

Peder Bjerre, archivist with Variety Corporation (Massey-Ferguson's successor), who provided background and photos.

David Crippen, Joan Klimchalk, Cynthia Read-Miller and staff of The Ford Museum Archives at the Henry Ford Museum and Greenfield Village, who patiently dug out the black and white pictures appearing in this book.

Andrew Morland, photographer par excellence, who took the color photos (he made picture taking look easy, but I know it's not).

Michael Dregni, editor, and the others at Motorbooks International who put this work in print and bravely took the financial risk.

Like an overgrown gravestone, this 8N's nameplate signals the end of the senior Henry Ford's control of the Ford Motor Company, and the end of the famous Handshake Agreement that launched the N Series tractors. Very little time was spent on restyling the 8N to differentiate it from its predecessor, the 2N. About all that was done aesthetically was to eliminate the Ferguson System badge, add the Ford script and change the paint from all gray to a lighter gray for the sheet metal and red for the castings.

The Handshake Agreement

"You haven't got enough money to buy my patents," Harry Ferguson bluntly told Henry Ford. Ford was, by the by, possibly the richest man in the world at that time, 1938.

"Well, you need me as much as I need you," retorted Ford, "so what do you propose?"

"A gentleman's agreement," explained Ferguson. "You stake your reputation and resources on this idea, I stake a lifetime of design and invention—no written agreement could be worthy of what this represents. If you trust me, I'll trust you."

"It's a good idea," said Ford. And with that the two men stood and shook hands.

Thus was born an agricultural concept that would revolutionize farming. Not only is the squat, compact, insectlike tractor, with its integral implements, still very much in evidence more than fifty years later, but virtually every farm tractor built since the patents ran out or could be circumvented has embodied the Ford Tractor's principal element: the three-point hitch.

Until mid 1947, the correct name was Ford Tractor, Ferguson System or Ford-Ferguson. The similarity between Ford-Ferguson and Fordson, which was built by Ford in the United States between 1917 and 1928, caused considerable confusion.

Further complicating matters, in 1947 Ford abrogated the Handshake Agreement and began producing tractors without Ferguson. Ferguson then manufactured his own tractor, which was so similar that many recognized no difference. Suddenly there were Fordsons, Ford-Fergusons, Fergusons and Fords. Many old-timers still refer to them all as Fordsons.

Messrs. Ford and Ferguson had remarkably similar backgrounds, characters and temperaments. Both were Irish. Both were raised on farms—Ford in Michigan, Ferguson in Ireland. Both had a love for the land, a sympathy for

Harry Ferguson explains the workings of his System. On a kitchen table brought outside for his historic meeting with Henry Ford in 1938, Ferguson used a model to show how increased draft forces increased traction without the risk of back-flip accidents. Ford was so impressed that he entered into the now-famous Handshake Agreement with Ferguson on the spot. Together, they plunged into the development of the 9N Ford-Ferguson tractor.

The Fordson Model N of 1932 owned by Brian Poole of England. This tractor has the water washer air cleaner.

farmers and their problems, a love for mechanical things and a disdain for the horse. Both had an almost mystical charismatic leadership ability that allowed them to enlist the extremely talented and loyal employees who made their businesses succeed.

Ironically, Harry Ferguson probably had more to do with the acceptance of the Ford Tractor than did anyone, including Henry Ford. It was the Ferguson System of implement integration that changed the tractor from a replacement for the horse to a truly useful and productive tool.

Harry Ferguson, left, appears with Henry Ford at the 9N introduction demonstration on June 29, 1939. This was a mere nine months after the Handshake Agreement that initiated the tractor—an incredibly short time by today's standards. Ford and Ferguson, both charismatic geniuses, complemented each other in temperament and worked together to get things done. Note the 8x32 tires; 10x28 tires did not become standard until 1942. The overall diameter is the same, but the later version has better flotation and traction. Except for the tires and the grille change in mid 1940, the appearance of the Ford Tractor changed little through 1952.

Emerson Borneman's working 8N, near Byron, Illinois, is typical of thousands of Fords that are soldiering on while their contemporaries and competitors have long since been relegated to the role of antiques. Seventy-three-year-old Borneman said, "If I couldn't have an 8N, I'd quit farming."

10

Heritage: The Fordson

In 1939, the entire history of the tractor spanned barely thirty years. Although traction engines had been around since the mid-nineteenth century, the origin of the word *tractor* is credited to two men named Charles of Charles City, Iowa: Charles Hart and Charles Parr.

In 1906, Hart and Parr made the first successful internal-combustion gasoline traction engine and called it a tractor. These early Hart-Parrs and other steam and internal-combustion traction engines were immense machines, weighing 10,000 to 80,000 pounds. Such monsters were useful only in large fields, and mostly for plowing or as prime mover engines for driving machinery via flat belts. The small landowner, common to most of the world's agriculture, was stuck with horses, mules or oxen.

But animal tillage was painfully slow. A team of horses could plow about two acres per day, and that took all the energy of a good plowman as

The Fordson's low weight, weight distribution and simple implement hitch resulted in a severe pitch-up, or back-flip, problem. The front wheels tended to lift when the plow contacted a solid object such as a buried rock. Despite ignition cutouts and clutch-disengaging accessories, about 150 fatal accidents had been recorded by the time this 1924 model hit the fields. The extended fender wing on this example was a block (of sorts) to back flips. This photo of Palmer Fossum's 1924 Fordson shows the way the engine casting was bolted directly to the transmission-axle housing for the first truly frameless design. This design is credited to Eugene Farkas, Ford's chief tractor engineer. Farkas may have been influenced by the Wallis Cub, with its one-piece belly pan structure supporting and protecting the main components.

well. Besides the sheer effort of man-handling the plow all day was the attendant job of harnessing and un-harnessing the team, rubbing them down and generally tending to their needs. The biggest drawback to animal power, however, was that each year, a team of horses themselves consumed the produce of five acres. This encroachment on the cash-producing acreage was particularly hard on the small farmer.

Henry Ford and the Fordson

Henry Ford grew up on such a small farm outside Detroit in the late 1800s. As his interest in automobiles developed, he also expressed a desire, as he stated it, "to lift the burden of farming from flesh and blood and place it on steel and motors." In the early 1900s, he began to build experimental tractors from automobile components. Just four years after the founding of the Ford Motor Company in 1903, Ford made his first experimental tractor. He referred to it as his Automobile Plow.

In 1915, Ford built his first tractor from scratch. He considered it his second tractor and so called it the B. It had a 16 horsepower, two-cylinder, horizontally opposed engine, a spur gear transmission and three wheels—two front drivers and one rear steerer.

The Model B was never produced. It did, however, gain enough publicity to let the world know that Henry Ford was interested in developing a tractor. Although no public announcement was made, many farmers looked to Ford to do for the tractor what he had done for the automobile with his Model T car. Taking advantage of this expectation, a group of entrepreneurs in Minneapolis—which did include a man by the

name of Ford—organized The Ford Tractor Company. While these businesspeople did actually build and sell a few tractors, they really anticipated a settlement with Henry Ford for allowing him to use his own name.

Such was not to be the case, however, as the crafty Ford was not that easily taken. For organizational reasons, Ford formed a separate company to manufacture his new tractor, taking his young son Edsel as a partner. The name of the new company was Henry Ford and Son and the name of the new tractor was the Fordson, leaving, for the time being, the Ford Tractor name to the Minneapolis outfit.

The Fordson was launched in 1916. It was the first lightweight, mass-produced tractor in the world, and for the first time, the average farmer could buy and own a tractor. The heritage of the Ford Tractor was set with the Fordson, which was built by Ford in the United States between 1917 and 1928 and in the United Kingdom until 1946. By the end of its production life, there were about as many American-built Fordsons as there would be 9N, 2N and 8N Ford Tractors.

The most revolutionary feature of the Fordson was that it lacked a con-

A well-dressed and dapper Henry Ford shows off his Automobile Plow in 1907. The term tractor had not yet come into common use, having been coined by Hart-Parr only the year before. Note the classic right-hand-drive car in the background, probably a six-cylinder Ford Model K.

In about 1907, just four years after the founding of the Ford Motor Company, young Henry Ford sits atop his Automobile Plow, so named because it was made from automobile parts. It featured a two-cylinder transverse-mounted engine, chain and gear drive, and magneto ignition.

Next page
The fender wings of Palmer Fossum's 1924 Fordson. Note the tool and storage spaces provided. The Fordson name was a contraction of the company name Henry Ford and Son. In 1915, the Ford Motor Company was a stock company. When launching his new tractor venture with his son Edsel, Ford no longer needed the financial assistance of, nor the limitations imposed by, stockholders, so the new company was privately held. By 1920, Ford had managed to buy out the Ford Motor Company stockholders, so Henry Ford and Son was folded into the parent company, but the Fordson name was retained.

Fordson—the first mass-produced farm tractor. Clearly showing its heritage of the later N Series Ford Tractors, this 1920 version poses for a publicity photo. Also shown is the frameless construction, where the housings of the engine, transmission and differential are bolted together to provide the structure of the tractor. The Fordson was rated at 20 horsepower on the belt and 10 horsepower on the drawbar.

Henry Ford and son Edsel are seen at a Fordson demonstration in 1921. When the Fordson tractor was introduced in 1916, the Ford Motor Company was not wholly owned by the Ford family. Chafing under the restrictions of a board of directors, Ford launched his new Fordson tractor through a new and separate company, Henry Ford and Son.

ventional frame. Instead, the cast-iron engine, transmission and axle housings were all bolted together to form the structure of the tractor. Within a few years, this feature was copied by others, and with the exception of garden tractors and the large articulated four-wheel-drive units, most have been made this way ever since.

The Fordson had a 20 horsepower, four-cylinder engine, a three-speed spur gear transmission and a worm gear reduction set in the differential. Because high-ratio worm sets generally transmit rotation from the worm element to the gear element, no brakes were provided on early Fordsons. All you needed to do to stop was depress the clutch. The reason for this one-way rotation phenomenon is simply the efficiency, or rather the lack of efficiency, of worm gear sets. The sets used in the Fordson were about fifty percent efficient. This meant that of the 20 horsepower the Fordson's engine produced, only about ten survived passage through the worm set; the other ten came out as heat.

The initial version of the Fordson had the worm set right under the driver's seat, and after short periods of operation, the heat on the bottom of the driver became unbearable. Subsequent versions saw the worm placed under, rather than on top of, the differential, where it ran submerged in oil. The problem of the hot seat was eliminated.

By 1917, World War I had Europe in upheaval. The British Board of Agriculture, fearing mass food shortages, sought ways to dramatically increase the amount of land tillage, even though the army was placing mounting demands upon available horses. Two Fordsons were imported for testing in June of that year, and the tests proved the Fordson to be reasonably well suited to the British terrain and soil. Because of this and the unique mass production features of the Fordson, the Lloyd George government called for immediate British production.

Henry Ford, although a pacifist, generously made a gift of the patent rights for the tractor and agreed to establish a factory in Cork, Ireland, the town from which the Ford family had emigrated. As a stopgap, 6,000 American-made Fordsons were imported

The heritage of the subsequent Ford Tractor is clearly seen in this view of Doug Zillmer's 1922 Fordson. Fenders were options, but necessary for the operator's safety. The general size and shape are similar to those of the N Series Ford Tractors. Note the steering wheel location and angle. The operator's semistraddle position is also reminiscent. The Fordson engine produced 20 horsepower at the belt pulley and 10 horsepower at the drawbar, bringing about the sometimes-used cognomen of Fordson 20-10. The rear wheels of the Fordson are proportionally farther forward than those of the N Series Ford Tractors. This was done for two reasons. First, it allowed the operator to reach the control handles on the trailing implements, which would otherwise have been farther back to clear the wheels in turns. Second, it put a higher proportion of the tractor's 2,700 pounds on the drive wheels. Nevertheless, traction was one of the Fordson's weakest points. The Fordson had the dubious honor of registering the lowest traction efficiency of the 60 tractors tested by the University of Nebraska in 1920.

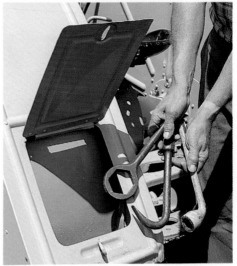

Palmer Fossum's 1924 Fordson has the original tool set supplied with the tractor. Total production of the Fordson reached 448,000 in 1924, and the 500,000th Fordson was built in mid 1925. The production price stabilized at about $400 (with the tool set).

until the Irish-made tractors began rolling off the production line. The few British tractor makers of the time reacted with considerable resentment. Importing and manufacturing the Fordson was the only logical choice for the government, however. No other way was available to reach the production volume required.

By 1928, when US production ended, 750,000 Fordsons had been produced. British production of the original Fordson concept, with refinements, continued until 1946.

The Fordson was, however, conceived merely as a replacement for a team of horses. Horse-type implements were attached to the tractor by a length of chain. The draft clevis was attached to the tractor's differential housing high enough for the implement to provide a downward pull to give added traction. This was common practice for tractors of that day, but it caused many back-flip accidents when the plow or other attachment hit an obstruction. Under these circumstances, the rear wheels could not slip, because of the downward pull of the implement, so the tractor reared up and flipped over backward. The high engine speed, the heavy engine flywheel and the inability of the wheels to slip caused the rearing action to be so rapid that drivers had no time to react. Often, drivers were pinned to the ground they sought to till.

Many farmers grew to hate the Fordson. Its name became synonymous with aggravation in agriculture. The reasons Fordsons became anathema were obvious and numerous. All machinery of that period lacked the considerable refinement found in the next generation, but these vehicles seemed to fail or attack their operators at the least convenient moment. In addition, many farmers had a relationship with their horses that stemmed from hours of toiling together. These agriculturalists hated to see the inevitable demise of horse farming and considered the Fordson a heartless substitute—which it was. Furthermore, many implements

This Dagenham-built 1938 Fordson Standard Model N, with oil bath air cleaner, works for owner Paul Matthews of Sturminster, England.

were made to be pulled by either horse or tractor, so the advantages of tractor power could not be realized. Finally, utilizing the full potential of the tractor engine's horsepower resulted in back flips, wheel slippage or damage to the implement.

Enter Harry Ferguson and the Ferguson System

Henry George "Harry" Ferguson was born in 1884, when Henry Ford was twenty-one years old. He was strong-willed, and had a penchant for confrontation with his father and schoolmasters. He left school at the age of fourteen to work on the family farm, where he came to hate the toil of agricultural work. In his late teens and early twenties, he worked for his

brother in the automobile business as a mechanic and race driver. He showed remarkable mechanical ability and possessed an innate engineering talent. He even designed, built and flew several monoplanes, just slightly behind the highly publicized activities of the Wright brothers from Dayton, Ohio.

Ferguson's most prominent attribute, however, was not his talent as an engineer, not his skill as a mechanic, not his bravery as a race car driver or airplane pilot; it was his high degree of perseverance. Ferguson's enduring claim to fame was his System: the integration of farm implements with the tractor. Through years of adversity, he stuck with his goal of perfecting and mass-producing his beloved System, which embodied principles

This example of the Dagenham-built Fordsons has the water washer air cleaner. Owner Keith Dorey of Wareham, Dorset, England, did the restoration.

found today on almost every farm tractor in the world.

"It is no more possible to design a plow which would be suitable for use with various sizes of tractors than it is to design a cart which can be drawn by a donkey or a Clydesdale, or a body that would be suitable for all makes of cars," Ferguson said, as he launched himself into the implement business. The first application of his System was a plow for the lightweight Ford/Eros tractor, which was a conversion kit for the Ford Model T car. It was made by a St. Paul, Minnesota, firm

20

Harry Ferguson demonstrates his Ferguson-Brown tractor in 1938. The Ferguson-Brown was manufactured as a joint venture of Harry Ferguson and David Brown. It was the production version of Ferguson's Black Tractor, which was the first to incorporate the hydraulic three-point hitch and integrated implements. The Ferguson-Brown was somewhat smaller than a Fordson, and cost about twice as much, but its performance was enough better that it convinced Henry Ford to build the 9N Ford Tractor featuring the Ferguson System.

The three-point hitch is found on the business end of the Ford Tractor. This Ferguson System hitch and the low price provided by Ford's mass-production ingenuity ensured the 9N's success. Shown here is Homer Clark's 1940 9N, serial number 38975, in the trailer hitch configuration. Implements connect to the ends of the two draft bars extending aft from under the axles and to the spring clevis above the differential housing, making the three points.

21

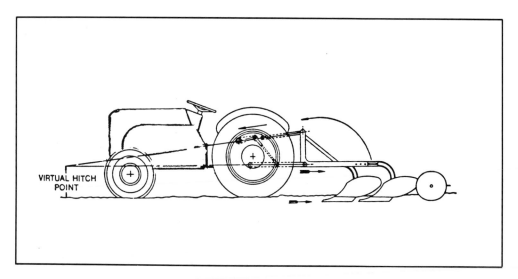

VIRTUAL HITCH
POINT

Several forces are at work with the Ferguson-designed automatic Draft Control.

and consisted mainly of larger rear wheels mounted behind the normal axle on a frame extension, a much increased gear reduction and increased engine cooling. The Eros performed and sold quite well, and the Ferguson plow was a popular accessory.

The Ferguson plow weighed less than half as much as a conventional plow. Its ingenious feature was the way it hitched under the belly of the Eros tractor, forward of the rear axle. Thus the pulling force—the line of draft—tended to draw all four wheels onto the ground. Excellent traction was provided and any tendency for rearing was eliminated.

Ferguson's first application for his System was doomed from the start, however, not because farmers didn't like the plow, but because the market for the Eros tractor rapidly dried up. For it was 1916, the year Henry Ford and Son launched the Fordson.

But perseverance was Harry Ferguson's long suit. Rather than fight the Fordson in the marketplace, Ferguson saw the vehicle as an opportunity to sell even more plows. At this time, the commitment had been made to build the Fordson factory in Ireland. Harry Ferguson learned that Charles Sorenson, Henry Ford's right-hand man for forty years, was coming to Britain to set it up. Plow drawings in hand, Ferguson rushed to London to meet with him.

"Your Fordson's allright as far as it goes," he reportedly said to Sorenson—and while he gained little in rapport with the man, he did at once get his attention. Ferguson's confidence, enthusiasm and aggressiveness carried the day. Charlie Sorenson lived to regret that first meeting, which ended with his commitment to support Ferguson's development of a plow for the Fordson tractor.

After considerable difficulty with some directors of his own Harry Ferguson Motors who simply wanted to adapt the huge inventory of Eros plows to the Fordson, Ferguson and his resident genius Willie Sands came up with a completely new System concept. Called the Duplex Hitch, the plow was coupled to the Fordson by two parallel links, one above the other, attached to the Fordson above and below the rear axle differential housing. Thus, draft loads pulled down on the rear wheels, but also pushed down on the front wheels through the upper link, thereby eliminating the rearing tendency.

This mounting must be considered semirigid, as there were no hydraulics to control depth or to raise and lower the implement. The arrangement was said to be no better than acceptable because there was no provision for maintaining a constant plow depth as the tractor's front wheels went over undulating ground. Nevertheless, Ferguson obtained a patent on the Duplex Hitch and later, a patent for a Floating

Skid device that tended to maintain the plow at an even depth.

Ferguson's next problem came from his inability to find suitable manufacturing arrangements in the United States. The plow was being produced, but not in high enough quantities to be profitable. Onto the scene came Eber and George Sherman of New York: Fordson dealers, entrepreneurs and confidants of Henry Ford. The Sherman brothers offered to team with Harry Ferguson to manufacture the plow with the Duplex Hitch in grand quantities.

Ferguson-Sherman Incorporated was established in 1925. Rumors that US production of the Fordson tractor would be halted by Ford began in 1926, and in 1927, the ax fell. The Fordson had ceased to be profitable and its factory space was needed for the new Model A car.

Draft Control

While Harry Ferguson was busy with the Sherman brothers marketing the Duplex Hitch plow, his research team was working on improvements. The main thrust was in the area of hydraulics: a mechanism to raise and lower the plow and to control tillage depth. In particular, depth control was still a problem. The Floating Skid patent worked well enough on the plow, but now the researchers were expanding the System to include other implements such as discs, harrows and cultivators.

The research team began working on the principle that pulling force, or *draft,* was proportional to implement depth, assuming constant soil conditions. Draft forces were reflected to the implement attach points so that when draft increased, the implement should be raised hydraulically until the original draft was re-established.

Consider, for example, the task of opening new ground with a plow. The plow is set to run approximately 8 inches in the ground. As the tractor moves forward over the uneven terrain, the front wheels encounter a hump that raises the front end and allows the plow to dig proportionally

This is how to change wheel treads on the Ford-Ferguson tractor.

THE FORD - FERGUSON TRACTOR

WHEEL TREADS FROM 48″ TO 76″ — QUICKLY, EASILY

● Fast, easy changes of wheel treads in 4″ steps from 48″ to 76″ makes the Ford-Ferguson Tractor a truly practical row crop tractor with all the advantages of four wheel construction.

One important time saving feature in changing treads is that no adjustment of steering linkage is required when front tread is changed. Diagram shows why. The axle ends move rearward as they are extended—distances between points where ends of radius rods and drag links are attached remain constant. Therefore wheel alignment always remains correct regardless of tread setting. This also makes possible offset front wheel for special work.

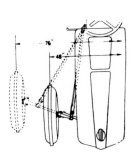

FRONT TREAD

● Center and end sections of the front axle are provided with a series of holes which permit the axle ends to be extended up to 72″ in 4″ steps. Change from 72″ to 76″ is made by reversing front wheels so disc is outward.

REAR TREAD

● The rear tread is widened by changing the position of the rims on the wheels in combination with changing or reversing the discs of the wheels, as illustrated below. Tread widths are possible from 48″ to 76″ in 4″ steps. Switch wheels, when necessary to permit tire tread to run in right direction.

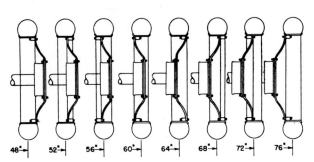

48″ 52″ 56″ 60″ 64″ 68″ 72″ 76″

EIGHT WHEEL WIDTHS IN 4 INCH STEPS
From

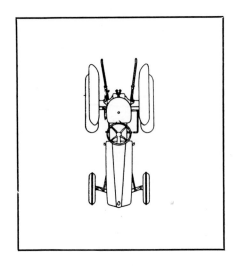

NARROW

48″ tread (52″ rear tread recommended for plowing and general work.)

To

W I D E

Up to 76″ tread for row crop work.

THE FORD - FERGUSON TRACTOR

FRONT AXLE

● The front axle consists of a center section, pivoted directly to the engine, and two axle ends. All three parts are alloy steel, designed for high strength. Axle ends are adjustable on the center section, each being fastened by two bolts. Tubular radius rods extend from the axle ends

to the transmission case to strengthen the axle against thrust forces. Cross section illustration shows the large vertical axle spindle and bushings provided for long wear. Spindle thrust is taken on an anti-friction bearing to make steering easier. Hub spindle is pre-packed for lubrication. Special thrust face seal prevents dust from entering and greases from leaking out.

STEERING

● To reduce steering effort and make the front wheels respond quickly when steering wheel is turned, a bevel pinion and twin bevel sectors are used. Each sector is linked independently to one of the front wheels. To minimize friction, the steering column is mounted on two tapered roller bearings. The 18-in. steering wheel is made of hard rubber with a steel core.

CLUTCH

● This semi-centrifugal clutch has two outstanding advantages. It is capable of transmitting much higher torque than the engine develops, and yet a light pedal pressure is maintained through the use of centrifugal weights.

The clutch is a single plate type and is composed of two major units, the pressure plate and cover assembly and the clutch disc. The pressure plate is arched and triangular shaped so as

to give correct ventilation which is vitally necessary for good clutch operation.

The steel clutch disc has friction facing rings riveted on each side. There are six crimped steel

segments interposed between one lining and the disc which give the required amount of cushioning to insure smooth clutch engagement and long life of the friction facing.

A mechanical dampener incorporated in the hub of the driven member serves to insure quiet operation of the transmission and absorbs the shock of sudden clutch engagement.

● In cutaway illustration, L is one of the three release levers with weighted outer end W. Levers are mounted on pressure plate by needle roller bearings B and attached to cover plate by flattened pin and roller R. As engine speed increases, centrifugal force causes weighted outer ends of levers to attempt to assume a position in the vertical plane passing through R, which increases pressure against the clutch plate P. This adds to the pressure exerted by the six clutch springs S.

Clutch disc diameter . . . . 9 inches
Friction area . . . . 75.3 sq. in.

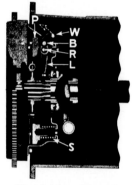

Both the clutch release bearing and pilot bearing are prelubricated type ball bearings and require no further lubrication.

● The clutch pedal works so easily that it can be operated by a small boy or girl. The long pedal provides increased leverage which reduces the pressure required. Clutch pedal and left brake pedal are side by side. The clutch pedal also applies the left brake when it is depressed past the point where clutch is completely disengaged.

No adjustment is required on the clutch other than to maintain a required amount of free travel in the clutch pedal.

Driveline specifics are given for the Ford-Ferguson tractor.

deeper. Instantly, as draft increases, the plow is lifted. As the front wheels drop off the hump, the hydraulics return the plow to its original position.

That is how it worked in theory. The task of the researchers was to come up with a simple, reliable and inexpensive way to accomplish this as rapidly as humps were encountered. They began their efforts using the Duplex two-point hitch arrangement. Draft forces were sensed in the bottom link. This worked well enough that in 1925, Ferguson obtained a patent entitled Apparatus for Coupling Agricultural Implements to Tractors and Automatically Regulating the Depth of Work, known simply as Draft Control.

Draft Control solved only part of the problem, however, as semirigid implement mounting aft of the rear axle also had lateral positioning problems. If, for example, the front wheels were steered to the left, the rear-mounted implement would swing to the right. In the case of a cultivator, this meant ripping out the very plants you sought to steer away from.

At this point, Ferguson's team realized that using two side-by-side lower links instead of just one would cause the virtual, or apparent, hitch point to be far forward of the actual attach points at the back of the tractor, so that the virtual lateral hitch point could be projected forward to the front axle. The two lower links now provided the draft, while the single upper link provided the download on the front wheels. All three links were equipped with ball joints on the tractor ends to allow for flexibility. The automatic Draft Control sensor was incorporated into the upper link.

In 1928, Ferguson began searching for a manufacturer to build a tractor incorporating his new three-point hitch. He did succeed in interesting the Morris Motor Company of England, but before the deal was signed, Morris canceled. The English firm had come to the same conclusion others were reaching, that world economic conditions were not good for new ventures. In 1929, Ferguson was again foiled by the stock market crash and the Great Depression.

The Black Tractor

Undaunted, Ferguson and his research team began designing their own tractor incorporating the three-point System. The hydraulics were to be built in, not just added on.

Interesting a manufacturer would be much easier, reasoned Ferguson, if he had a prototype to demonstrate. When the drawings were finished, he began contacting companies specializing in the parts required.

For the transmission and axle, the choice was the David Brown Company, a family-owned business that had begun in 1860 and grown into the largest gear producer in Great Britain. As it happened, that initial order began a chain of events that led to David Brown's becoming one of the world's foremost tractor companies, subsequently folded into Case/International Harvester. But in 1933, the David Brown Company was merely a parts supplier, one of several contributing to Ferguson's prototype.

Perhaps influenced by Henry Ford's "any color so long as it is black" philosophy, the prototype was painted black, and it was named the Black Tractor. Much testing and development was accomplished on this vehicle before satisfactory performance was realized. Eventually, David Brown committed to manufacturing the production tractor in a joint-venture company called Ferguson-Brown, Ltd. Sales were disappointing, however, because of the worldwide depression and because, although the love for them was largely lost, there were almost 800,000 Fordsons in the field. Switching to the Ferguson-Brown meant buying all new implements as well.

Nevertheless, Ferguson pressed on. In January 1938, one of his associates entered a Ferguson-Brown tractor in a comparative plowing demonstration at the Rowett Research Institute in Aberdeen, Scotland. Luckily, snow fell the night before the demonstration, and only the Ferguson-Brown (with its weight-transferring System) and a four-wheel-drive outfit were able to plow. Farmers went away amazed.

Still, sales were so low as to be unprofitable, and soon disagreement erupted between Brown and Ferguson. Brown wanted to build a bigger tractor; Ferguson wanted to increase production to the point where the price could be lower, building to inventory

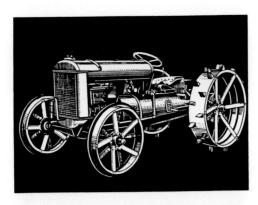

The 1933 Ferguson Black Tractor was the first prototype Ferguson tractor. It was named the Black Tractor simply because of its black paint scheme.

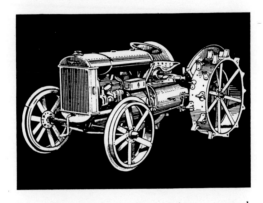

The 1936 Ferguson-Brown incorporated the Ferguson System with Draft Control.

until sales developed. When the two reached an impasse, Brown began making the changes he deemed necessary. In mid 1938, a frustrated Ferguson sailed for America to demonstrate his System to Henry Ford.

The Handshake Agreement

Henry Ford never intended for his company to be completely out of the tractor business when US production of the Fordson was halted in 1927. As hope returned to economic horizons, he began experimenting with new designs. He also kept in contact with the elder Sherman brother, Eber. The Shermans had continued in the tractor business by importing British-built Fordsons, and they were also involved with Harry Ferguson in building and marketing the Ferguson plow for the Fordson.

Not one to miss an opportunity, Harry Ferguson made sure that Eber

Sherman came to Great Britain early in 1938, to see a demonstration of the Ferguson-Brown tractor and implements. It was Ferguson's point of view in his disagreement with Brown that mass production was the key, and who knew more about mass production than Henry Ford. And how would Ferguson get to Ford? Eber Sherman, of course.

Sherman dutifully reported to Ford what he had seen. He suggested that Ford might be interested in the remarkable System. Of course Ford was interested, and Ferguson was invited to meet with him. Thus, in the fall of 1938, Ferguson and several aides brought a crated Ferguson-Brown tractor and implements by ship and truck to Ford's Fair Lane Estate.

It was a bright blue October day when the demonstration began. The tractor had been meticulously prepared. Only a small group was present: the Ferguson team, the Ford team, the Sherman brothers and the truck driver who brought the tractor from New York.

The demonstration was convincing. The diminutive Ferguson-Brown, about eight-tenths the size of a Fordson, clearly outperformed both a Fordson and an Allis-Chalmers with the same-size plows.

Ford took on a serious attitude and called for a table and two chairs to be brought out. Ferguson had a hand-sized model of the tractor, with which he was able to clearly explain his System to Ford as they sat at the table. The result of this conversation was a handshake, sealing a gentleman's agreement that Ford would make tractors and deliver them to Ferguson. Ferguson would have implements made by other sources to his designs and would be responsible for setting up dealerships and marketing. Further, it was agreed that either could terminate the agreement at will and without explanation.

From this Handshake Agreement, as it came to be known, came the immensely successful Ford Tractor. Also came much confusion about what the agreement covered and who was responsible for what. Nevertheless, as long as Henry Ford was in charge of the Ford Motor Company, the agreement worked.

This 1926 Fordson from the Fossum Collection has a homemade cab and is equipped with the Ferguson Duplex Hitch plow with its Floating Skid depth control device—the forerunner of the three-point hitch. US production of the Fordson ended in 1927 or early 1928, when the tractor's factory space was usurped by the new Model A car. Fordsons were also produced in Ireland and England, English production continuing until 1946.

The Tractors of the Century: N Series

Just three months after that bright blue October day of the Handshake Agreement, experimental models were ready for testing. Another six months saw completion of the 9N prototype, which incorporated all the important features. This prototype was taken to Fair Lane, where Messrs. Ford and Ferguson gave plowing demonstrations to a group of invited guests. Performance was spectacular, despite all the compromises Ferguson had to accept in order to achieve the mass production goals Ford required.

The Model 9N tractor

The 9N hit the dealer showrooms early enough in 1939 that over 10,000 were sold yet that year. The launch price of $585 included rubber tires; an electrical system with a starter, generator and battery; and a power takeoff. Headlights were optional.

The engine was a four-cylinder L-head type with 120 cubic inches of displacement, a 3.187 x 3.75 inch bore and stroke, and a 6:1 compression ratio, which produced 28 horsepower at 2000 rpm. Remarkable for its time, the tractor included as standard a large-capacity cartridge-type oil filter and an oil bath air cleaner. Also unusual for its time, but much appreciated, was an automotive-type reverse-flow muffler. Early Ford publications suggested the possibility of mounting a radio, because of the tractor's low noise level.

While most tractors of that day used magneto ignitions, the 9N had a direct-driven distributor with an integral coil. Magneto ignitions of the 1930s were cantankerous and troublesome and often induced kickback into the hand crank, resulting in many a broken arm. Needless to say, the mod-ern ignition system and self-starter were welcomed.

An ingenious front wheel tread adjustment adapted the tractor to the width of crop rows. The front axle consisted of a center section that overlapped two outboard stub sections to which the wheels attached. Radius rods from the tractor body held the axle in place, a practice typical of Ford cars in those days. Steering linkages ran parallel with the radius rods down both sides of the tractor. The center and end sections of the axle were provided with a series of holes and two bolts for each side. The angle of the center section allowed the axle length to be varied by changing the amount of overlap, without the need to change, or even detach, either the radius rods or the steering linkages. This feature was not found in the 8N or subsequent Ford tractors; apparently, it was a concession to Ferguson patent claims.

Rear wheel tread could be changed by changing the position of the wheels on the rims and by reversing the wheel discs.

The key feature of the tractor was the Ferguson System. The three-point hitch allowed eighteen different implements to be either attached or

Note the 8x32 rear tires on this 1939 Model 9N Ford-Ferguson, serial number 364; size 10x28 tires became standard equipment in 1942, and 11.2x28 and 12x28 tires can also be used. Note also the horizontal grille spokes reminiscent of Ford car and truck grilles of the period. This grille type was made of cast aluminum and was used until 1941. The new grille, with vertical spokes, was made of steel, as aluminum was rapidly becoming a strategic war material.

This 1939 Ford-Ferguson 9N, serial number 364, owned by Palmer Fossum of Northfield, Minnesota, is a beautiful example of the earliest version of the classic Ford Tractor. Significant features include a cast-aluminum hood, grille and dashboard. Harold Brock of Waterloo, Iowa, a former Ford employee involved with developing the tractor, told Fossum that cast-aluminum hoods were used on the initial batch because stamping equipment for steel was not ready in time. The aluminum hoods and grilles proved to be quite fragile and have largely been replaced over the years.

Henry Ford introduces the new 9N to the press in June 1939. Besides plowing demonstrations given by himself and Harry Ferguson, Ford had the eight-year-old boy standing by the tractor show the ease with which the tractor and plow could be handled. To the amazement of the crowd, the boy's furrows were as straight and even as those of experienced plowmen like Ford and Ferguson. Note the identifying features of the early Ford Tractor: the smooth rear axle hub, cast-aluminum horizontal-spoke grille, four-spoke steering wheel and squarish manifold casting.

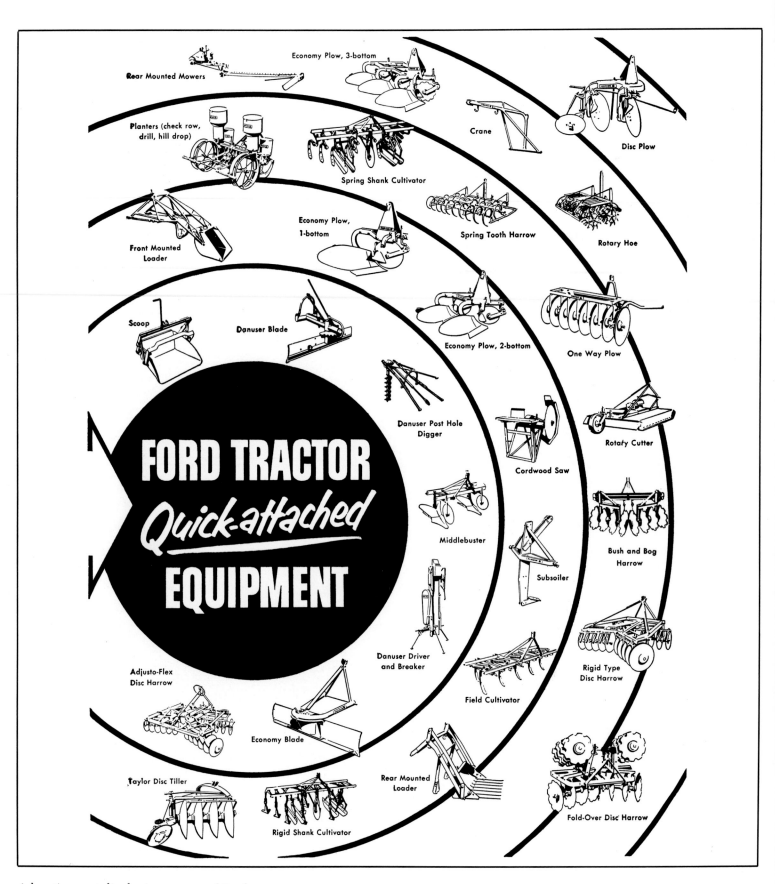

Advertisement displaying a range of Ford
Tractor equipment.

removed in about a minute. The hydraulic system enabled the tractor to carry an implement to the field and then to regulate its working depth with the patented Draft Control.

To say that the 9N was a success would be an understatement. The model's low price, about half that of equivalent tractors, alone accounted for some of its acceptability. Before World War II, some 17 million horses were still employed in agriculture. Farmers had ceased to question the cost-effectiveness of the tractor versus the horse, but the usurpation of production capacity by World War II kept down the number of 9Ns sold. Then, in 1942, after producing 99,002 Model 9Ns, Ford changed to the 2N version.

The Model 2N tractor

The pedigree of the 2N has more questions than answers. Opinions vary as to what differences there were between the 9N and the 2N, and why the model designation was changed. Until the subsequent 8N, model numbers were not commonly used in identifying the Ford Tractor. Only in parts catalogs were the differences noted.

Some authorities now speculate that the 2N designation simply indicated the incorporation of changes that improved life, reduced cost or simplified assembly. Others state that the 2N, correctly designated 2NAN, was a wartime kerosene-burning version, of which most examples have since been converted to gasoline. The most believable assessment appears to be that the 2 indicated 1942, and the 2N was introduced as a stripped-down wartime version with steel wheels and no electrical system. Then, as the wartime materials situation eased, the configuration more or less reverted to that of the 9N.

In today's parts catalogs, there are no parts indicated as being peculiar to either the 2N or the 9N. Identification can be made by serial number, or by the 9N's lack of the external hood-side panel attach fasteners found on 2Ns and 8Ns just ahead of the front axle, and by a four-spoke truck-type steer-

Harry Ferguson shows his plowing skill at the 9N press introduction in June 1939. The event was organized by the Ferguson-Sherman company at Ford's Fair Lane Estate. In typical Ferguson fashion, it was a well-planned gala event. Several new tractors were on hand with various Ferguson-Sherman implements. An area was fenced off so the 9N could demonstrate how well it operated in tight corners. The day's festivities for the 500 invited guests included a lunch served under large tents.

ing wheel found on most 9Ns. Otherwise, there are no visible differences between the 9N and 2N.

It was Ford's policy to incorporate changes and improvements throughout the year as necessary, but mostly at year-end. Accordingly, different configurations appear within the model designations, as well as within year-models. For example, the original 9Ns, introduced in 1939, have characteristics not found on later tractors:

• The instrument panel contains a starter button near the ammeter, the

Henry Ford, Harry Ferguson and the Sherman brothers, Eber and George, right to left, appear with the 9N prototype. The Sherman brothers joined Ferguson in manufacturing implements for the 9N and in setting up the dealer organization. Their relationships with Ford and Ferguson went back a long way. The Shermans had been Fordson dealers and the principal importers of Fordsons after US production was halted in 1927. They had also been in business with Ferguson building his two-point hitch plow for the Fordson. Notice the lack of name badges on the front of the tractor, although a place for the Ford emblem has been cast into the hood. Also notice the rear tire, between Ford and Ferguson; it seems to be a solid rubber type, with the tread attached by fasteners.

key switch near the oil pressure gauge and a red light to indicate when the ignition is on.
• The rear axle hubs are smooth.
• The front axle radius rods are I-beam type.
• The battery/fuel cap cover is not hinged, but is a snap-in-place type.
• Front axle grease fittings are on the forward side.
• The grille has semihorizontal spokes.
• The steering sector box, battery holder, grille, transmission covers, instrument panel and sometimes the hood (on the earliest models) are cast aluminum.

• The rear fenders have two crease bars instead of one.
• The left and right brake pedals are identical and interchangeable.
    The 1940 9N has several different features:
• A safety interlocked starter is introduced midyear.
• A hinged cover is used for the battery and fuel cap.
• A three-brush generator is installed.
    The 1941 9N incorporates these changes:
• The left brake pedal is now different from the right.
• Front axle grease fittings are moved to the rear for protection.

34

• A steel grille with vertical bars appears.
• A three-spoke steering wheel is introduced midyear.

In 1942, the designation was changed to 2N. Peculiarities of this year-model are as follows:
• The 10.00x28 rear tires become standard.
• The steering wheel is changed to a three-spoke with steel rod spokes.
• A pressurized radiator is introduced.
• A nonelectrical, steel wheel version with magneto ignition, hand crank starter and front choke is made available to save war-critical materials and keep production up.

In 1944, the last of the visible changes were made when the radius rods were changed to an oval tubular section and sealed-beam headlights were incorporated. Of course, some internal and construction method changes were made as time went on.

When this happened, for the most part, the old parts were dropped from the catalog. Hence, by now, most tractors have been updated to the latest configuration.

Models 9N and 2N summary

The original Ford Tractor (9N or 2N) weighed about 2,300 pounds, was painted a solid Forest Gray (darker than the 8N gray) and could work all day on 10 gallons of gas. It has two drawbacks: its brake pedal/clutch pedal placement and its three-speed transmission. Apparently, the engineers felt it more natural to put the left and right brake pedals on the left and right sides of the tractor. The clutch pedal is located on the left side with the left brake. Depressing the clutch fully also operates a linkage that actuates the left brake pedal. This is fine for stopping—you simply depress the clutch and right brake pedals. The

Palmer Fossum astride serial number 364, a 1939 Model 9N Ford-Ferguson. The four-spoke truck-type steering wheel was used through 1941. Besides carrying a full line of new and used parts for Ford tractors, Fossum is probably the number one Ford collector. He has over 50 Ford Tractors in his collection, including at least one of every year-model from 1924 to 1959. He also has a rare 1941 Ford pickup truck with a factory-installed Ford Tractor four-cylinder engine.

problem comes when a tight left turn is required from a stop. You must first release the clutch before using the left foot to actuate the left brake, and by then you are often already into the fence.

The limitations of only a three-speed transmission were largely overcome when the Sherman brothers

The 9N engine, shown here from the left side, was a four-cylinder L-head with a 3.187x3.75 inch bore and stroke, 119.7 cubic inches of displacement and a 6:1 compression ratio. It produced 28 brake horsepower at 2000 rpm bare, and 24 horsepower at the belt pulley with muffler, fan and generator installed. Note the original I-beam-type radius rod. The 1939 engines had no freeze plugs, so this must be either a 1940 or 1941, as a freeze plug is visible behind the oil filter.

introduced their Step-Up auxiliary transmission. Space was available between the clutch housing and the transmission, with a convenient split line at that point, which allowed the installation of a direct and high-range gear set—and, subsequently, a set of low-direct-high-range gears. With one of these auxiliary Shifters, the right ratio for the job could be found. Road speed was increased from 12 mph at 2100 rpm to almost 18 mph. However, with the step-down (low-range) version, torque and bearing loads on the transmission, differential and rear axle can exceed design limits. In addition, torque at the rear wheels is great enough that back-flip accidents when pulling from the drawbar (not the three-point hitch) have to be guarded against.

Exit Henry Ford

By 1945, frail, eighty-two-year-old automotive pioneer Henry Ford resigned and his grandson, Henry Ford II took his place. By then, it had become obvious to many in Ford management that Ferguson held the clean end of the agreement stick. Much of the risk and investment were in the tractor end of the bargain. And, while tractors were provided to Ferguson at a fixed price, Ferguson did not offer a fixed price through the dealer network. He could raise both the price of tractors to dealers and the price of implements. Ferguson also stood to profit most from the sale of parts and service.

In late 1946, Henry Ford II told Ferguson that the Handshake Agreement would end in mid 1947. Ford also announced a new, improved version of the tractor with a complete new line of Ford-produced implements. A whole new dealership organization was to be set up, independent of Ferguson.

The new tractor, the Model 8N, hit the dealer showrooms in July 1947. It was an immediate success, with almost 40,000 being produced by the end of the year.

Ferguson's reaction was twofold. First, with remarkable speed, he set up a manufacturing operation to make his own tractor, the Ferguson TO-20. In appearance, it was a dead ringer for the Ford 2N, even to the paint color,

but improvements made it comparable to the new 8N. Second, Ferguson launched a $340 million lawsuit against Ford for patent infringement and for damages caused by loss of business.

Six years later, in 1952, the suit was settled with an award to Ferguson of just less than $10 million. Over 200 lawyers had taken part, trying to sort out the complexities of the Handshake Agreement. The main militant against Ferguson's case was the success of his new tractor. It belied the damages-for-loss-of-business claim. Ford made some changes to the 8N to evade the patents, but the settlement was mainly for infringements. The next Ford trac-

tor, the 1953 Model NAA Jubilee, had major changes in the hydraulic system and other areas, as ordered by the court.

The Model 8N tractor

The new Ford 8N introduced in July 1947 was a classic engineering masterpiece. A 1948 model (hence the 8N designation), it was one of the most popular tractors ever produced. Improvements over the 9N and 2N models were numerous.

A slightly more powerful engine was used, with the compression ratio increased from 6:1 to 6.5:1. Otherwise, the engines were basically the same.

In 1939, a one-piece intake-exhaust manifold was used on the 9N engine, shown here from the right side. The generator was a simple shunt-wound type with a vibrator voltage regulator. In 1940, this was changed to a three-brush and cutout type.

Later, a side-mounted distributor and separate coil were provided, replacing the integral unit under the fan.

A four-speed transmission—a much-needed improvement—added greatly to the tractor's flexibility and productivity. First and second overall ratios were the same as before. These

Previous page
Homer Clark and this 1940 9N have been farming together for 50 years. Back in 1940, the National Farm Youth Foundation (NFYF) and Ford-Ferguson dealers awarded 29 new tractors as prizes in tractor operation and plowing contests. The contests were held in each of the 29 sales districts. Clark won this tractor, serial number 38975, in the Fond du Lac, Wisconsin, district. The Clark farm is in LaValle, Wisconsin, near Madison.

A line-up of transport trucks is loaded with 9N Ford Tractors. This photo was taken January 16, 1940, on the streets of Dearborn. The large number of tractors shown represents only about half of one day's production. The other half were probably shipped by railroad. Henry Ford determined the size of the tractor in order to fit the maximum number into a railroad car. The sign in the radiator grille of the lead truck, a 1939 Ford COE, reads, "Taxes paid by motor transports help keep down the taxes on your car."

In June 1940, a pair of 9Ns teams-up with a 1940 Ford truck to do some harvesting. The aluminum grilles were quite fragile; some were reportedly fractured by tall stubble.

were considered to be already ideal, first being selected on the basis of drive component strength and tire traction, and second being the best for pulling a two-bottom, 14 inch plow through normal soil. Third and fourth gears were on both sides of the old high gear. Third was the drag-harrowing gear; fourth was the road gear. Reverse was the ratio equivalent of third gear, rather than of first as on the 9N–2N transmission. This provided much faster back-ups, but also meant a lot of clutch slipping when maneuvering backwards in tight quarters. The Sherman-type step-up, step-down shifter found a useful home on the 8N despite the new four-speed gearbox.

In addition to automatic depth control (an original feature of the Ferguson System), the new 8N included Position Control lever under the seat. The purpose of this control was to block out depth control and cause the implement to remain at a constant position relative to the tractor regardless of the draft load. This was a great convenience for such implements as the grader blade, cultivator, box scraper and so on. Draft Control was used for tillage implements where depth of work automatically varied according to draft forces.

After 1947, the top link rocker, which actuated the draft sensing mechanism, contained three moment arm positions rather than the previous one. This allowed macro adjustments in Draft Control sensitivity.

Although the brake mechanism for the 8N was improved over the 9N–2N system, the big news was that both

A 9N has the wheel and fender removed to show the three-point hitch mechanism. The control lever quadrant is beside the seat. Behind the seat is the leveling crank, which lengthens or shortens the right-hand draft link strut. Below the leveling crank is the Draft Control spring, against which draft forces work. If draft force increases to the point where the spring is compressed, the hydraulic control valve is actuated to raise the implement in the same manner as if the control quadrant lever were raised. When the obstacle is past and draft forces return to normal, the spring repositions the hydraulic control valve and the implement returns to its normal working depth. The tractor shown is a mid 1940 model, photographed on June 7, 1940. Note the safety interlock starter button, the hinged battery/fuel cap cover, the I-beam-type radius rods from the transmission case to the front axle and the smooth rear axle hubs. The Ferguson two-bottom plow is shown in the fully raised position.

pedals were now on the right side, positioned so that both could be depressed simultaneously for stopping or individually for maneuvering.

In terms of steering improvements, a new recirculating ball mechanism replaced the previously used sector gear setup. This resulted in reduced steering friction and backlash and provided for longer life. Steering wheel angle and height were also both increased on the 8N.

The new 8N was basically the same size and shape as the 9N and 2N, but it had light gray sheet metal and

An early 8N Ford Tractor is doing what it does best—plowing. Although over 400 implements would eventually be available, the Draft Control three-point hitch worked its best with the two-bottom plow. Many farmers of the forties plowed several hundred acres per year with 8Ns.

Early tractors, through 1941, incorporated significant changes throughout the model years. Features of the 1940 Model 9N were the hinged battery/fuel cap cover, an improved voltage regulator/generator and a safety starter button that was mechanically interlocked with the transmission lever in neutral.

Previous page
Homer Clark's 1940 9N was built late enough in the production year to include the midyear changes such as the safety interlock starter and the three-brush generator. Clark has also made some later-configuration changes to update his tractor. Because of the looming shadows of World War II, little was done in exporting the 9N. However, Canada, Cuba and Mexico each had one of the 38 Ferguson-Sherman distributors.

wheels with dark red cast iron. Accordingly, it soon picked up the nickname Red Belly. Also new were an air cleaner grille as well as red Ford scripts on either side of the hood and later also on the insides of the fenders. After serial number 290,271 in late 1950, 8Ns contained a multifunctional panel instrument that displayed engine revolutions per minute, ground speed at different gear selections and engine operating hours.

By the end of production in December 1952, 524,076 Model 8N units were produced. Over 400 implements were offered through the Dearborn Motors subsidiary. Besides those already mentioned, numerous other minor improvements increased life, ease of use or ease of repair. The price stayed amazingly low throughout production, eventually rising to about $1,200 in 1952.

Homer Clark's 1940 9N has a new grille of the later type, as the original aluminum grille was broken in a tornado.

Next page
This is a 1941 9N. The chrome trim around the ammeter, left, the oil pressure gauge, right, the shift knob, the choke button and the radiator cap would all disappear from the next year's model, the wartime 1942 2N.

An early 1941 9N shows off its front-mounted snowplow and other features, including a new grille with vertical spokes, a larger generator, the nonsmooth rear axle hubs, liberal use of chrome and a Ford emblem trimmed in chrome on the front of the tractor. The snowplow was operated through cables from the lift arms of the three-point hitch, so the operator used the same control lever as for rear-mounted implements. A 1941 Ford car stands in the background. Behind the car are classic examples of the period's residential architecture.

The year 1942 was one of fairly major changes and saw a change in designation from 9N (signifying 1939) to 2N (1942). This 1942 2N Ford-Ferguson from the Fossum Collection has no electrical system, but has a magneto ignition and steel wheels. Tractors were considered essential war items, but production was only 16,487 2Ns in 1942, down from almost 43,000 in 1941 because of wartime shortages. Production of the tractor without rubber tires or copper in the starters and generators helped keep numbers up. Production reached 21,000 in 1943 and 43,000 in 1944, and most examples had tires and electrical systems by then, showing that material problems were largely overcome as the war progressed.

52

A BNO-25 Aircraft Tug, a variation of the 2N, does its thing with a B-24 Liberator. This picture was taken in March 1943, at the Willow Run airport, where Ford manufactured a record number of Liberators during World War II. The BNO-25 had a single brake pedal, no three-point hitch and heavy sheet metal. Another version, the BNO-40, had dual rear wheels. The rated drawbar pull was 2,500 pounds for the BNO-25 and 4,000 pounds for the BNO-40. With an empty weight of about 36,000 pounds, the Liberator was probably quite a load for the BNO-25.

Ford Tractors come off the assembly line at the Rouge Plant in 1944, some of the 43,443 built that year.

81664

A 1945 2N Ford-Ferguson demonstrates Ferguson's ingenious self-jacking system, which was operated by the three-point hitch hydraulics. The Jacking System was introduced to allow rapid adjustment of wheel spacing.

The handsome art deco styling is apparent in this photo of Leroy Folkerts' 1946 Ford-Ferguson. Styling was done by the Ford car styling department, and reflected the image of Ford cars and trucks.

Leroy Folkerts atop his 1946 2N Ford-Ferguson. Although this tractor is restored to showroom condition, it still does some work on the Folkerts' acreage. The 1946 model has all the improvements incorporated in the 9N and 2N; no improvements were made in the 1947 model. Over 97,000 2Ns were made in 1946 and 1947, so they are the most prevalent of the 9Ns and 2Ns.

Leroy Folkerts' 1946 Model 2N, serial number 225015, was one of some 59,000 Ford-Fergusons produced that year. The 9N–2N design was reaching maturity. Although the production rate was fairly steady, reaching a high of nearly 37,627 in the first six months of 1947, a major update was clearly required to keep the tractor competitive. Even with the subsequent 8N, Ford was never able to best International's Farmall for the number one sales spot. International had a line of tractors from small ones equivalent to the Ford to large diesel models. The idea for a tractor line of several sizes seems to have eluded Ford until 1954.

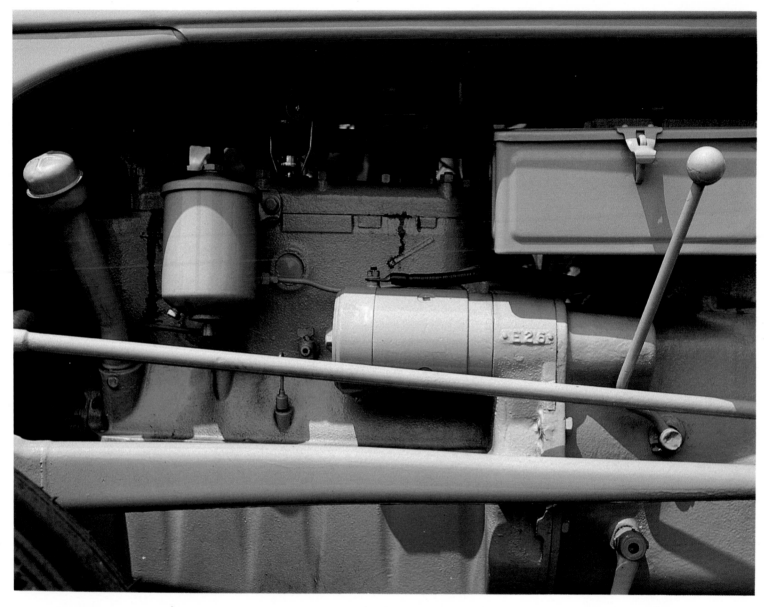

Previous page

This 1946 Ford-Ferguson belongs to Leroy Folkerts. Ford wiped out the competition for tractors under 30 horsepower with the 9N, 2N and subsequent 8N, but a lot of the competition's tractors were selling in the over 30 horsepower class, which kept Ford in the number two sales spot. However, the Ferguson System, with its penchant for improving traction, made a Ford with a plow perform as if it had 10 more horsepower.

This left side view of Leroy Folkerts' Ford-Ferguson 2N engine shows the shift lever for the Sherman Step-Up transmission, which greatly improves the flexibility of the Ford Tractor. The Sherman gives six forward speeds rather than three, and improves road speed from 11 mph to almost 18 mph. Putting the Sherman in neutral also allows operation of the engine without the power takeoff and hydraulics, and makes for easier cold weather starting by reducing the load on the starter (if the clutch is engaged). The 119.7 cubic inch engine was basically one half of the 239 cubic inch V-8 used in production cars and trucks. The original concept was to use production pistons, rods and so on, but in practice the tractor parts had to be beefed up a bit. The starter motor was interchangeable with that used on the small 60 horsepower V-8.

60

Leroy Folkerts owns this 1946 Ford-Ferguson. The Ford N Series tractor was made lower to the ground than contemporary competing tractors. While this was at least a perceived drawback for row crop farming, it was necessary for safety. When an implement, such as a plow, was raised, the overall center of gravity was considerably higher. A spin turn at the end of a row that was rapidly stopped by straightening the front wheels, and even applying the opposite brake, imparted a considerable roll couple. Add to this hillside conditions and the possibility of simultaneously dropping into a furrow, and the need for a low, squat stance is obvious.

Leroy Folkert's 1946 2N has the optional high air cleaner intake shown just ahead of the steering wheel. The standard intake was under the hood, where it was exposed to an extra amount of dirt thrown by the front wheels and fan. The optional intake was expected to receive cleaner air above the hood. There is a fine screen under the cap to keep out bigger particles, while the regular oil bath tank, below, takes out dust and dirt. Notice the new Ford accessory seat cushion. The standard metal seat leaves a lot to be desired in terms of comfort. The seat is adjustable by removing the attachment nut and moving the seat to a different hole in the seat spring.

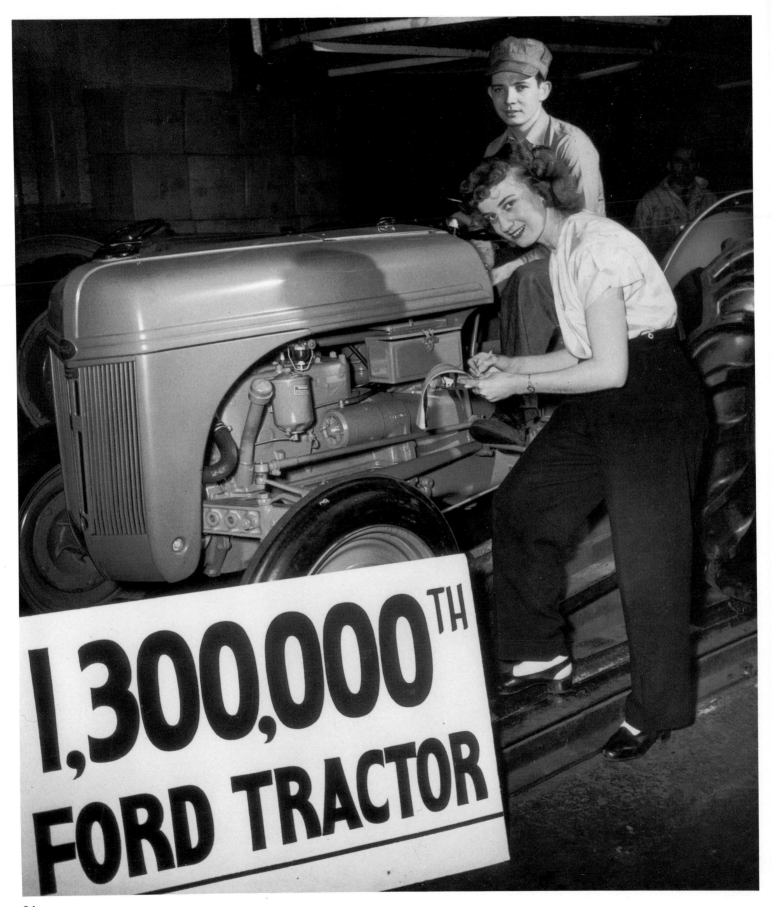

On April 4, 1947, the 1,300,000th Ford-built tractor rolls off the Rouge line. The number includes 739,977 American-built Fordsons and some 300,000 British-built Fordsons. Production of 2Ns was nearing an end; in July 1947, that model would be replaced by the new 8N.

In July 1947, the first new 8N rolls off the assembly line at the Ford Rouge Plant. Although it looked much like the 2N it replaced, the 8N had a more powerful engine, an improved hydraulic system, better brakes, a new steering system, running boards and other refinements. A lighter

gray paint for the sheet metal contrasted nicely with bright red castings. Chrome appeared around the Ford logo on the front and the Ferguson System badge disappeared. Also new was the Ford script on the hood, and later on the rear fenders.

This 1947 Ford-Ferguson 2N Sugar Cane and Cotton Special from the Fossum Collection is a unique conversion that was popular in Louisiana and other southern states. It was designed to be a competitor for the Farmall F-12 and F-14 and the Case RC. The rear tires are 9x40s with special fender risers for clearance. The front tire is a 10x12.

The rear wheels of Fossum's Sugar Cane and Cotton Special have slots in the rims so that spacing can be changed. The wagon is a Ford Dearborn model.

FORD HYDRAULIC TOUCH CONTROL
includes constant draft feature

Lifting or lowering of implements is handled anywhere at any time without effort, just by touching the hydraulic control lever. An implement can be lowered to desired working depth and under uniform soil conditions, this depth will be automatically maintained.

Crossing a grassed waterway.

Lifts, lowers and controls implement in the ground at the touch of a finger.

Plus Ford Hydraulic Touch Control

Maintains uniform depth under varying soil conditions.

FORD HYDRAULIC TOUCH CONTROL
includes Implement Position Control

This great new Ford advancement means smoother operation, less wear on tractor and driver, easier, better work. In fields with reasonably smooth surfaces all you do is set the controls once—and uniform working depth of implements is automatically maintained, even when soil conditions vary.

See Your Dealer. Your nearby Ford Tractor dealer asks you to remember that he is headquarters for genuine Ford Tractor parts and for implement and tractor service second to none. He is a good man to know.

A 1947 ad presents the Ford Hydraulic Touch Control.

The classic 8N Ford Tractor with a Dearborn Implement box scraper. When Ford and Ferguson went their separate ways in 1947, Ford marketed its own line of implements under the trade name Dearborn Implement Company. The box scraper works much like the old horse-drawn slip scraper, except the tractor and three-point hitch do the hard work. Most versions of the box scraper can be turned around, so they can be filled while backing. Thus, they can be used to dig from a bank or in similar situations where you can't drive over the ground to be excavated.

Next page
A 1947 ad for Ford Tractors displays the three-point attachment.

Ford TRACTOR

FORD TRIPLE-QUICK ATTACHING

Saves time here to use in the field.

You can attach or detach most implements in a minute or less. Arrows above show 3-point, triple-quick attachment. Even such a job as changing from mower to cultivator, or cultivator to mower, is easily done in 10 minutes.

Quick, Easy Attachment of Implements

ADD UP TO FASTER, EASIER FARMING

There will always be plenty of work to do on any farm . . . but there's no reason why as much of this work as possible shouldn't be made as fast and easy as possible.

This was the idea that Ford engineers had in mind when they went at the job of designing this great new Ford Tractor.

How well they succeeded is being proved every day now, as more and more farmers get an opportunity to see this new tractor, to put it through its paces, to turn it loose on their own farms.

That great combination—Ford Triple-Quick Attaching, and Ford Hydraulic Touch Control—is the last word in simplifying tractor operation, saving time both in barnyard and field, and in assuring you a better job with less work. You'll only need to try this combination once to realize how far ahead it is.

Owners of this new Ford Tractor are finding plenty more to talk about, of course. There's the new 4-speed transmission—four forward speeds and reverse, giving better selection of speeds to fit the work, and faster top speed. There's new, easier steering and improved braking. There's a total of 22 worthwhile advancements, each doing its share to make the new Ford Tractor a *better* tractor— and a better investment for you.

Your Ford Tractor dealer invites you to examine this new tractor and the many quality implements that have been designed especially to work with it. He'll be glad to demonstrate both tractor and implements to you.

We think you'll agree that your farm work *can* be made faster, easier and more productive—the new Ford Tractor way.

DEARBORN MOTORS CORPORATION, DETROIT 3, MICHIGAN

Dearborn FARM EQUIPMENT

Dearborn Farm Equipment includes a wide variety of quality implements, specially designed by qualified implement engineers to operate with the Ford Tractor and field tested by practical farmers. Ask your Ford Tractor dealer to demonstrate them on your farm.

Marketed and serviced through a national organization of Dearborn Motors Distributors and Ford Tractor dealers.

COPYRIGHT 1952 DEARBORN MOTORS CORPORATION

NEW 4-SPEED TRANSMISSION gives you the advantage of a fourth forward speed, with stepped up top speed for road travel and faster operation in other speeds. New helical gears are in constant mesh, for easy, quiet shifting. Transmission cover plate is easily removable.

NEW BRAKE PEDALS, both mounted on right side. Either right or left brake can be operated with the right foot, or both operated together, leaving foot free for clutch. New Duo-servo type brakes give positive braking on either or both rear wheels.

NEW HYDRAULIC TOUCH CONTROL and linkage save both your time and your muscle. Implements are easily and quickly attached or detached. New attachment lugs plus provision for installation of swinging drawbar, permit more efficient use of a wide variety of equipment.

NEW SCREENED AIR INTAKE is conveniently located where dust is at a minimum. Has vented grille easily removable for cleaning. Special air cleaner extension (available as accessory) for use in extremely dusty conditions, is easily attached without drilling a hole in hood.

NEW AUTOMOTIVE TYPE STEERING GEAR provides steering ease comparable to your car. On turns, wheels hold true with minimum steering effort. Mechanism is readily adjusted for wear. This easier steering makes a big difference in a long day's work.

NEW SPRINGY, HINGE-BACK SEAT tilts up and back, giving you the relief of standup operation when desired. New 24" x 7" step plates, asbestos shielded on muffler side, provide foot comfort, make it easier, safer to get on and off.

A Quality Line of Basic Implements

Several of the implements now in the Dearborn line are listed at the right. Many more are being developed and will be ready soon. You will want Dearborn Implements because they are specially designed to operate with the Ford Tractor, and are of quality construction throughout. Expert implement engineers have designed them and practical farmers have thoroughly tested them.

Most Dearborn Implements may be attached or detached in a minute or so and take full advantage of Ford Hydraulic Touch Control for safe, easy transport to and from the field and almost effortless control of operation. Ask your Ford Tractor dealer for literature on implements now available, and watch for announcement of additions to the line.

Dearborn

FARM EQUIPMENT

- Moldboard Plow
- Disc Plow
- Rigid Shank Cultivator
- Rigid Shank Front End Cultivator
- Spring Shank Cultivator
- Spring Shank Front End Cultivator
- Single Disc Harrow
- Tandem Disc Harrow
- Rear Attached Mower
- Four Row Weeder

- Cordwood Saw
- Scoop
- Utility Blade
- Angle Dozer
- V Snow Plow
- Blade Snow Plow
- Front End Loader
- Sweep Rake
- Heavy Duty Loader
- 4 Wheel Wagon
- Post-Hole Digger

and many others

See Your Dealer.

Your Ford Tractor dealer is Ford Farming Headquarters in your locality, with all that this means in faster farming and less work and more income per acre. See him for a new tractor, for implements, for parts, for expert, on-the-spot service and for helpful suggestions. He is a good man to know.

MARKETED AND SERVICED THROUGH A NATIONAL ORGANIZATION OF DEARBORN MOTORS DISTRIBUTORS AND FORD TRACTOR DEALERS

Previous page
A 1947 ad showcases tractor features.

The half-track kit was a popular after-market accessory for both Fords and Fergusons. Besides this set made by Bombardier, the Canadian snowmobile and aircraft company, and installed on a 1948 Ford 8N owned by Fossum, the Arps track was also widely used. The additional traction and flotation are phenomenal. Operators report that the difference is like that between two- and four-wheel-drive. Although the tracks can be used for fieldwork, they are made for use on snow, mud or muddy concrete, such as for cleaning out a cattle yard with a front loader. The half-track can nicely handle the front snowplow implement and is also much in demand for use in maple sugaring.

A 1949 ad shows the line of implements.

This classic 1950 Ford 8N with a factory canopy was purchased new by Palmer Fossum's father on March 10, 1950. This was the tractor that infused Fossum with a love that has caused him to become a foremost collector of Ford Ns. The five-bow Ford accessory top has special brackets that fit on the fenders. The top is attached to the brackets with wing nuts; thus, it can readily be folded back, or removed when not in use. Besides being a desirable shield from the blazing sun, the canopy was also welcome when sudden rain showers came up.

Although the classic 8N appears to be longer and heavier than its predecessors, it is basically the same size and shape. The length, 115 inches, was supposedly set by Henry Ford himself, to fit the maximum number of tractors on a rail car. Ed Pochinski of Hatley, Wisconsin, has restored this mint 1951 8N over a period of years, obtaining parts and assistance from Strojney Implement Company, Ford-Ferguson specialists in Mosinee, Wisconsin.

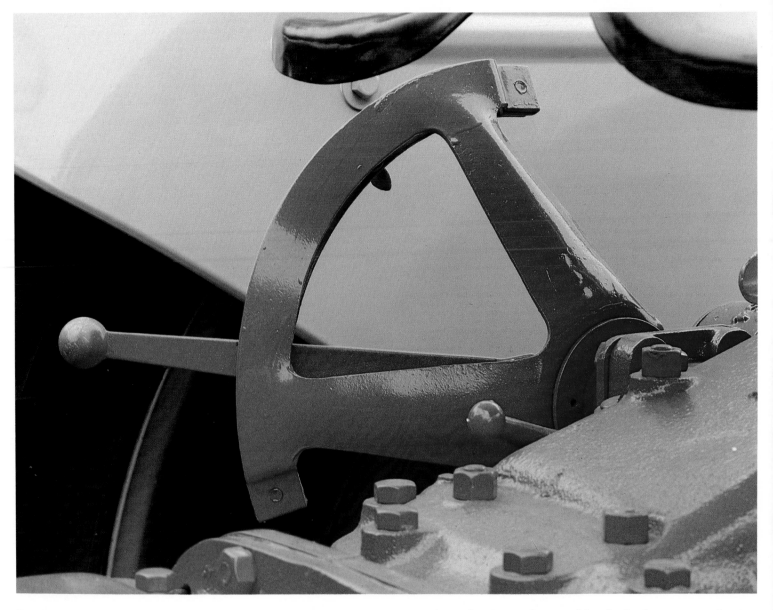

Previous page

The Ford operators manual describes the 8N as follows: "The Ford two-bottom plow tractor is of the four-wheel type construction. A wide range of wheel spacings are provided. The short wheelbase and low over-all height give it greater flexibility and maneuverability. Implements are easily attached to the tractor by means of the 3-pin mounting."

One improvement incorporated into the 8N was the addition of Position Control to the previously available Draft Control. The Position Control lever is the small lever barely visible between the main control quadrant and the transmission housing. The hydraulics operate in the Position Control mode when the lever is in the vertical position, and under Draft Control when horizontal. Draft Control is commonly used with tillage tools, such as a plow. The implement will run at the set depth as long as the soil is uniform, but will rise or fall as draft forces increase or decrease. Position Control holds the implement at a constant position relative to the tractor, regardless of draft loads. Scoops, grader blades and grain drills are examples of tools that need Position Control.

A 1951 ad for the Ford Tractor emphasizes power and low cost.

TOP PRODUCTION!...
WITH LESS HELP!...AT LOW COST!

THE WHOLE FAMILY HELPS—Any member of the family can be a full-fledged tractor operator with a Ford Tractor. Triple quick-attaching of implements and Ford Tractor Hydraulic Touch Control make this possible.

GET MORE OF THE CROP—With no extra equipment the Dearborn-Wood Bros. Combine's header operates from 2 to 38″ off the ground, to get lodged, low growing or rank crops. Big capacity. Bin, bagger models; PTO or Ford Farming Engine powered.

Ford Tractor POWER is Helping Thousands of Farmers Do Their Biggest Job

American farmers know what all-out production means. Long hours of work. Less and less help. Making use of every possible acre of soil and of every tool that will help to get the job done faster and better. Men coming out of retirement and getting back into the fields. Young people and women pitching in and doing the work of grown men.

This is the way the job was done before. It is the way it will have to be done now—in 1951.

To do more jobs and save more hours, Ford Tractors and Dearborn Implements, specially engineered to work with them, form an unbeatable combination. On farms short of help, the Ford Tractor which anybody, young or old, can use is a priceless "hired man." And on *any* farm, the handy, economical Ford Tractor can be a big factor in keeping production *up*, costs *down*.

We shall continue to do our best, through the nation-wide organization of Ford Tractor dealers, to help American agriculture do its biggest job.

LOW FIRST COST—LOW OPERATING COST The low priced Ford Tractor has a remarkably low operating cost, too. The Proof-Meter (see arrow) not only proves this fact but permits you to cut costs still further.

Previous page
Most 8Ns are not county fair or parade items, but day-to-day working tools. This 1951 Model 8N, owned by Art Preston of Mauston, Wisconsin, is doing its duty with a mounted Dearborn hay rake. Art Preston is a retired Ford tractor dealer. It is not likely that this 8N will retire for a while yet.

The 8N tractors after serial number 290271 had an additional instrument in the panel: the Proof Meter. This was basically a time-recording tachometer with bands around the perimeter showing ground speed in the various gears and power take off revolutions per minute.

"Ford Farming" was the key phrase in the ad campaign introducing the 8N. It was printed on radiator grille covers and sold to owners for the purpose of keeping their radiators clean. This Ford accessory radiator grille cover is shown installed on Fossum's Sugar Cane and Cotton Special, a 2N conversion.

Ford and Ferguson Go Their Own Ways

Ferguson TE-20 and TO-20

Back in 1917, Henry Ford generously made a gift of the patent rights of the Fordson tractor to the British to help alleviate the World War I food supply problem. He also agreed to set up a factory for Fordson production in Cork, Ireland, under the operation of Ford's British subsidiary. In addition, Ford declared that he would take no profits from tractors made for the British government. The Ford subsidiary was practically an autonomous entity with a British board of directors, several of whom were in the government's Food Production Department.

In 1933, tractor production was moved to Dagenham, England, while the Cork facility was used to manufacture automobile components. According to Harry Ferguson, the Handshake Agreement of 1938 included the intention to stop Fordson production at Dagenham and begin British production of the new joint-venture tractor. Ferguson also understood that there would be a place for him on the British board of directors.

This was not to be the case, however, as the Ford directors in England would not go along with a model change

Strojney Implement's 1949 Ferguson TO-20 was Ferguson's answer to the 8N. When the Handshake Agreement between Ford and Ferguson was severed, Ferguson hastily set up manufacturing facilities for a US version of his English TE-20. The TO-20 was much the same, except for a US electrical system and some different casting materials. Although the Ferguson looked like a dead ringer for the Ford, very few parts interchange. Supposedly, Ferguson did this on purpose, to thwart the use of Ford parts in his tractors.

from the Fordson. Why not? Perhaps because of the wartime situation they faced, or perhaps because of the favorable royalty arrangement with the parent firm or perhaps because Fordsons still had a good market that they didn't have to share with products of the US factory. It was also quite likely that the directors were reluctant to work with the crusty Harry Ferguson, who, besides having the ear of Henry Ford, had a reputation for demanding his own way about everything.

Ferguson eventually accepted that the new tractor would not be made by the British Ford company and that there would not be a seat for him on the British board of directors. Accordingly, he began planning the manufacture, in England and under his own name, of a 2N-like tractor designated the TE-20.

One might wonder what Henry Ford thought of this undertaking. The truth is that he wasn't aware of it until it was a fait accompli. Henry Ferguson had sent him a letter outlining his pique with the British board of directors, but an aide to Ford had filed the letter without showing it to him. "We've got enough trouble making this Handshake Agreement work without this," the aide reasoned.

As soon as World War II ended, Ferguson negotiated a manufacturing agreement with Standard Motor Company. Production of the TE-20 began in late 1946 at the Banner Lane factory in Coventry, England.

The TE-20 was basically the same as the Ford-Ferguson 9N and 2N, but it had two important differences: an overhead-valve engine and a four-speed transmission. Additional minor changes and improvements included a pedal for the left brake on the right side

This 1948 Ferguson TE-20 with a Ferguson manure loader and spreader is from the Fossum Collection. Typical of the Ferguson genius, the spreader is equipped with a short stand under the tongue and a ring-type hitch. The tractor has an open hook attached to the drawbar. One could hook and unhook the spreader from the tractor without leaving the seat by lowering or raising the drawbar with the hydraulics. Thus, the tractor, with loader, could be used to load the spreader, and then to pull it to the field.

The 1949 TEA-20 owned by C. R. Middle-brooke of Otley, Yorkshire, England, is an agricultural show model; note the chrome steering wheel spokes and emblem. The shift lever and other parts are also chrome plated. The tractor was photographed at the Great Dorset Steam Fair.

The Ferguson TO-20's tilting hood allows easy access to many components otherwise obscured on the Ford. It does, however, preclude the use of most aftermarket loaders and bumpers unless specifically designed for the Ferguson. Some Fergies have had holes cut in their hoods for access to fuel and water caps when this tilting feature is blocked by a loader.

of the tractor as well as one on the left. A one-piece hood arrangement was also added with hinges at the front so that the whole assembly—grille and all—could be tilted, exposing everything from the radiator to the instrument panel.

In late 1946, Henry Ford II told Harry Ferguson that the Ford-Ferguson agreement would be abrogated in July 1947. This meant that Ferguson's

implement company, and his dealers, would be left out in the cold. The result was Ferguson's $340 million lawsuit and his decision to build a factory in Detroit to manufacture a US version of the TE-20, to be known as the TO-20.

It wasn't until October 1948 that Harry Ferguson drove TO-20 serial number 1 off the Detroit assembly line. The TO-20 was identical to the TE-20, except that it used a Delco ignition sys-

tem in place of the Lucas on the Continental Red Seal engine and it used cast iron rather than aluminum for the transmission housing. Aluminum was used in the TE-20 to better dissipate the combined hydraulic and transmission heat load; British oils of the time were less capable of higher operating temperatures than were US oils.

The TE-20 and TO-20 tractors quickly became a success. They were reliable and were priced competitively with the new Ford 8N. The TE-20s were imported throughout 1948 and 1949 until Detroit production of TO-20s could fill the demand.

One reason for the ready acceptance of the Ferguson was the fierce brand loyalty of owners in that period. If you were a Ford person, you wouldn't be caught with a General Motors

This 1951 Ferguson TEF-20, owned by R. B. Jones of Dorset, England, is powered by the quiet and smooth-running Freeman Sanders diesel engine. Freeman Sanders was an outstanding diesel engine designer. His improved combustion chamber design of 1935 resulted in cleaner exhaust and smoother running.

product on your place. Conversely, a farmer with Chevrolet cars and trucks wouldn't buy a Ford tractor even though he needed one. The appearance of the Fergies, as they came to be known, solved this dilemma for many farmers.

Because of their reputation for reliability, quite a number of Ferguson TE-20s found their way to Antarctica under the auspices of a British exploration program. Three of these vehicles, equipped with special tracked running gears, carried a Sir Edmund

Hillary expedition on a 1,200 mile trip to the South Pole.

The TO-20 was made in Detroit until the end of 1951. During 1951, the TO-30 was introduced and coproduced. This was basically the same tractor with a more powerful Continental engine and larger front tires.

Today, many Fergies are in routine use. The British-built TE-20s are becoming quite rare in the United States, although parts are generally available for all types through Massey-Ferguson dealers or tractor parts companies. Parts are not readily available for the TE version's Lucas electrical system, but by now, many tractors have had the Lucas system replaced by the Delco.

Ford NAA Jubilee

When the Ford-Ferguson lawsuit was settled in 1952, Ford engineers

had already been planning an improved tractor for introduction in 1953—Ford's fiftieth anniversary. Competition from the Ferguson TO-30, brought out in 1951, had been taking its toll on sales of Ford 8Ns. In addition, the lawsuit had made it obvious that a new hydraulic system would be required. And indeed, the court did decree that after 1952, Ford would have to use a completely different hydraulic control system.

Production of the new model, the NAA, began in January 1953. Prominent on the hood of the restyled tractor was a circular emblem that said Golden Jubilee Model 1903-1953, and the NAA quickly became known as the Jubilee. *Golden* referred to the fiftieth anniversary of the founding of the Ford Motor Company in 1903. *Jubilee* is a biblical term having to do with fifty-year periods (see Leviticus 25:11). (It is interesting to note that during the Jewish Year of Jubilee, there was to be no cultivation of the land.)

The Jubilee was somewhat larger and heavier than the 8N it replaced. Front and rear tread adjustments were accomplished in the same way and to the same extent, from 48 to 76 inches. The Jubilee had a 4 inch longer wheelbase, was about 4 inches higher and weighed about 100 pounds more.

Other than changes to the hydraulics, the most important improvement was the new Ford Red Tiger engine, an overhead-valve unit with 134 cubic inches of displacement and a 6.6:1 compression ratio that produced 31 horsepower at 2000 rpm.

The Ferguson lawsuit prevented the continued use of the old hydraulic pump with its supply-side control valve covered by Ferguson patents before the Handshake Agreement. In the old arrangement, the pump and control were under the seat in the transmission/differential housing. The pump was driven by the power takeoff mechanism only when the PTO and clutch were engaged.

The new pump was a vane type rather than the scotch-yoke type previously used. It was mounted on the right rear side of the engine, driven by a helical gear on the rear of the camshaft. Thus, hydraulic power was available whenever the engine was operating.

On top of the pump was a manual pump volume control called the Hytrol. This allowed smooth draft load sensing and smooth control of the three-point hitch with a variety of implements.

Also new on the Jubilee were a separate, independent hydraulic reservoir and outlets for providing hydraulic power to remote cylinders. A separate control valve was offered as an option.

A nonlive power takeoff was retained on the Jubilee as standard, but a continuous, or live, PTO was offered as an option. To provide the live PTO, a hydraulically actuated clutch was incorporated in the PTO drive. A separate pump was provided to actuate the clutch, driven by the Proof Meter cable.

AN IMPORTANT MESSAGE
TO OUR CUSTOMERS AND FRIENDS

We are happy to be able to tell you that the lawsuit brought more than four years ago against Ford Motor Company and Dearborn Motors Corporation by Harry Ferguson and Harry Ferguson, Inc. has been settled by agreement of the parties.

There are three points connected with this settlement which, as a present or possible future owner of a Ford Tractor, we want to make clear to you. Regardless of what you may hear to the contrary, these are the FACTS.

3 POINTS OF INTEREST
To Our Present and Future Customers

1 Ford Motor Company will continue production of the present Ford Tractor without interruption, and Dearborn Motors Corporation will continue to market them nationally as in the past. By the end of 1952, Ford Motor Company has agreed to make two simple changes, and only two changes, in the means of operation and control of a pump used in the hydraulic system in the Ford Tractor. After these simple changes have been made, there is nothing in the settlement of the suit to prevent Ford Motor Company from continuing the manufacture of the present Ford Tractor for as long as it may choose.

2 Ford Motor Company will continue to produce and Dearborn Motors Corporation will continue to supply, through its distributors and dealers, all repair parts for all past, present and future Ford Tractors.

3 Ford Tractors will continue to offer all the advantages of the present system of hydraulic control, the present method of attaching and operating implements, and all other features responsible for their wide popularity. Dearborn Motors will continue to offer its same complete line of implements.

A STATEMENT
By Mr. Henry Ford II

"In normal times Ford Motor Company would carry such a suit to a final conclusion in the courts. These are not normal times. Under the circumstances we were glad to get rid of the litigation to avoid the expense, harassment, and further interference with our tractor business involved in additional years in the courts.

"The settlement in no way interferes with Ford Motor Company's continuing to offer to the farmer the lowest priced tractor with hydraulic control and the present method of attaching and operating implements."

DEARBORN MOTORS CORPORATION, Birmingham, Mich.
National Marketing Organization for the Ford Tractor and Dearborn Farm Equipment

The Jubilee retained the recirculating ball steering gear and brakes of the 8N, as well as the 6 volt electrical system. The transmission was still four speeds, but the ratios were different. The reverse ratio was the equivalent of second gear, instead of third as on the 8N or first as on the 9N and 2N. Although 4.00x19 front tires were standard as on previous models,

A June 1952 ad from Ford announces the settlement of the Ford v. Ferguson lawsuit.

One man's faith in Justice makes this date memorable...
April 9, 1952

YEARS AGO a dream came true for Harry Ferguson. He obtained a patent on a device he had created—a hydraulic device that was to enable one man to do the work of many on the farms of America.

OTHER PATENTS were issued to this man, patents on devices that ended back-breaking farm tasks—that saved time and money. So good were these devices that eventually, by a handshake agreement, a large motor car company manufactured a tractor equipped with them. It was marketed as the Ford Tractor with Ferguson System,

integrating tractor and implement into one efficient machine.

AS SOMETIMES HAPPENS, this arrangement terminated and Harry Ferguson, Inc. made and marketed its own tractor using the Ferguson System. The Ford Tractor continued to be made and sold, embodying some of the Ferguson patents and inventions.

THUS HARRY FERGUSON found himself in competition with his own creations. He believed deeply in justice and in the rightness of his claim against the Ford Motor Company. It was this man's faith in these things that found justification on this date . . .

April 9, 1952

ON THIS DATE the United States District Court for the Southern District of New York entered a final judgment, with the consent of all parties which ended four years of litigation between Harry Ferguson, Inc. and Ford Motor Company and others.

IN THIS ACTION, it was ordered and adjudged that:

1. The sum of $9,250,000 shall be paid to Harry Ferguson, Inc. as royalties on Patents Nos. 1,916,945; 2,118,180; 2,223,002 and 2,486,257.

2. Ford Motor Company shall not manufacture, after December 31, 1952, such tractors, and Dearborn Motors Corporation shall not sell any such tractors manufactured after December 31, 1952, as have
(a) a pump having a valve on its suction side, as for example in the present Ford 8N tractor, arranged to be automatically controlled in accordance with the draft of an implement, or
(b) a pump for a hydraulically operated draft control system

for implement control and a power take-off shaft both driven by the lay shaft of the transmission, as for example in the present Ford 8N tractor, or
(c) a coupling mechanism on the upper portion of the center housing, of the form employed in Ford 8N tractors manufactured prior to November 22, 1949; and Ford Motor Company and Dearborn Motors Corporation must affix a notice on any long coupling pins, manufactured by them, to the effect that the pin is sold only for replacement on 8N tractors made by Ford prior to November 22, 1949. This notice will continue to be affixed until October 25, 1966.

3. Ford Motor Company and Dearborn Motors Corporation shall have a period of time, expiring not later than December 31, 1952, in which to make these changes.

4. All other claims and counterclaims are dismissed and withdrawn on the merits.

A COPY OF THE CONSENT JUDGMENT is available to anyone interested in reading it. This settlement between Harry Ferguson, Inc. and the Ford Motor Company resolves the issues. The inventions mentioned above with which this action was concerned will be found only in the Ferguson Tractor and in the Ferguson System in the future.

Harry Ferguson, Inc.

Detroit 32, Michigan

A June 1952 ad from Ferguson concerns the lawsuit's settlement.

In Jones' TEF-20, diesel power replaces the Continental engine of the original TE-20. Much historical data on the early Ferguson tractors is available from Keith Oltrogge, publisher of Wild Harvest, Massey Collectors News, a bimonthly newsletter for Wallis, Massey Harris and Massey-Ferguson collectors and enthusiasts, and from Peder Bjerre, archivist with Varity Corporation.

A Ferguson TE-20 on half-tracks works in Antarctica. Sir Edmund Hillary used Ferguson tractors on his historic expedition to the South Pole in 1958, and three Fergies made the round trip from the base camp to the pole. The altitude exceeded 9,000 feet, leaving the tractors with such limited power that the governors were reset to allow operation to 3600 rpm. Nevertheless, the Fergies performed flawlessly on the 1,200 mile trip. Hillary cabled back: "Despite quite unsuitable conditions of soft snow and high altitudes our Fergusons performed magnificently and it was their extreme reliability that made our trip to the Pole possible." The half-track running gear is still common for both Fords and Fergusons, especially in snow country. There are two main types: Bombardier and Arps.

6.00x16 tires were an option. These and other larger tires are almost universally found on Jubilees today.

Jubilees were made in 1953 and 1954. In 1955, they were replaced by the Model 600, which was essentially the same but without the Golden Jubilee emblem.

Beginning Jubilee serial numbers were NAA 1 in 1953 and NAA 77475 in 1954.

Later models

In early 1955, Ford announced five new tractors in two power classes, the 600 and the 800. Thus ended the era begun in 1917 wherein Ford was a single-tractor producer, and thus began the era wherein Ford would compete across the board. Liquified petroleum gas engines became an option later

that year for US tractors, and the Fordson Major Diesel was introduced in England.

The Workmaster and Powermaster lines—the 601 through 901 Series—were brought out in 1958, and later in the year came the 501. Each line had subseries numbers like 861, which indicated such things as the number of transmission speeds and whether or not the PTO was live.

American-built diesel engines also became available in 1958. First available was the 172 cubic inch four-cylinder engine. In 1961, a six-cylinder 242 cubic inch diesel engine was introduced in the five-plow Model 6000.

Today, Ford offers a complete line of tractors from riding mowers to huge articulated monsters. Throughout the intervening years, Ford tractor dealers have always carried an equivalent to the 9N-2N-8N. A Ford Model 1720 would be comparable to the 8N in horsepower and size, although it has a three-cylinder diesel engine, live hydraulics and a live PTO. It is also available with four-wheel-drive and with a hydraulic shuttle transmission, which allows selection of forward or reverse in any of the twelve speeds. If the $12,000 price tag is too much for your budget, however, your Ford tractor dealer is a good place to start looking for a true Ford Tractor—a 9N, 2N or 8N.

This new Jubilee hood emblem is available from Strojney Implement stock. The original emblems on the 1953 Ford Model NAA tractors had the words Golden Jubilee Model 1903-1953 written around the edge, signifying the fiftieth anniversary of the founding of the Ford Motor Company in 1903.

POWER *that Pur-r-rs*

when the going gets TOUGH!

NEW FORD TRACTOR

Golden Jubilee MODEL

POWER TO PULL 3 PLOWS
The new Ford Tractor will pull three bottoms in many soils. Its extra power speeds discing, tilling, subsoiling and other heavy field work, too.

Hitch the new Ford Tractor to a heavy pull and listen to its deep-throated pur-r-r as it buckles down to the job.

Watch its reserve of power surge into action when called on to start heavier loads and pull through tough going. Notice the smooth, even flow of power at all speeds. See how the engine actually seems to be loafing under normal loads . . . but watch the work it turns out!

Then you'll *know* that here is a new kind of tractor power—power

delivered only by Ford's new overhead valve "Red Tiger" engine. Due to reduced engine friction more of the tractor's power goes for pulling. And with the travel of each piston *reduced approximately 5 miles* in a working day, many hundreds of hours are added to engine life.

There are many, many more out-in-front features in the new Ford Tractor, all available to you at a low Ford price. It's worth a trip to your nearby Ford Tractor dealer to find out more.

DEARBORN MOTORS CORPORATION • Birmingham, Michigan
National Marketing Organization for the Ford Tractor and Dearborn Farm Equipment

LOOK WHAT YOU GET!

★ Most advanced hydraulic system in any tractor...Live-Action with Hy-Trol

★ Extra power... with Ford's great new "Red Tiger" engine

★ New hydraulically operated Live PTO*

★ New size, weight and ruggedness

★ A new high in comfort, convenience, safety

...And a LOW FORD PRICE, too

Ford Farming MEANS LESS WORK ...MORE INCOME PER ACRE

*Sold Separately

Leroy "Bud" Peterson aboard his 1954 Ford NAA Jubilee in Northfield, Minnesota. The Jubilee reflects the competitive and legal pressures brought on by Harry Ferguson. Besides the lawsuit, competition from the TO-20 and then, in 1951, the TO-30 caused Ford to make almost a complete redesign for its new NAA model.

An ad shows the Ford Golden Jubilee tractor with Red Tiger overhead-valve engine.

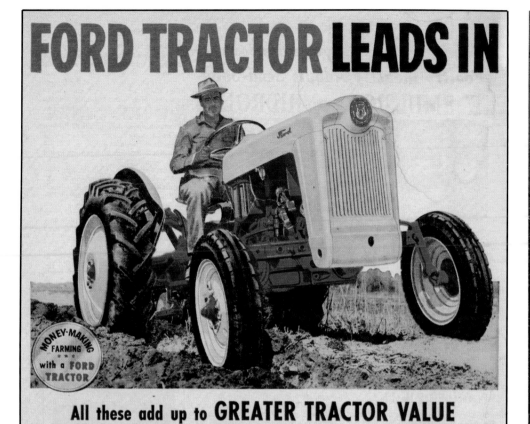

FORD TRACTOR LEADS IN

MONEY-MAKING FARMING with a FORD TRACTOR

All these add up to GREATER TRACTOR VALUE

FORD'S GREATEST TRACTOR ENGINE
Gives New High in Performance

You get more lugging power, longer engine life and exceptional fuel economy with Ford's new "Red Tiger" engine. Makes heavy field work go faster. In many soils, for example, the new Ford Tractor pulls three bottoms.

EXTRA HYDRAULIC POWER...
Most Advanced System in Any Tractor

Increased lifting power of Ford's new Live-Action Hydraulic System helps to handle bigger implements and heavier loads. In addition, you have a choice of hydraulic speeds and convenient attachment for remote cylinders.

PROOF OF PERFORMANCE
No Other Tractor Gives You

Only the Ford Tractor has the Proof-Meter. It is five useful instruments in one—shows hours worked, travel speed, belt and PTO speeds, and engine r.p.m. Helps you get top performance and more economy from your Ford Tractor.

Proof is Yours for the Asking. Let your nearby Ford Tractor Dealer show you the facts about power at low cost. See how easily this tractor, and the Dearborn Implements designed to work with it, handle the work you want done. See how quickly you can change from implement to implement and job to job, how much you can get done and, when you figure it all out, how much less you pay. We think you'll agree that today's Ford Tractor is your best buy in power and all around value.

 Ford TRACTOR

Dearborn EQUIPMENT

An ad presents the new Ford tractor.

By 1956, Ford was no longer a one-tractor producer. Late 1954 saw the introduction of the 600, 700, 800 and 900 Series tractors. These were quickly followed in 1957 by the 501, 601, 701, 801, 901 and 1801 Series. The Fossum Collection's 1956 Ford Model 660 shown here is essentially the same as the Jubilee, with minor improvements. It was the top of the 600 Series line, having a five-speed transmission and a live PTO. Other models in the series were the 650 with the five-speed and no live PTO, and the 640 with a four-speed like the Jubilee's and no live PTO.

Robert Breitrick is at the controls of this 1956 Ford Model 800 owned by Scott Breitrick of Tigerton, Wisconsin. The Model 800 has 45 horsepower, enough to do most jobs on a family farm without too much overkill. It has live hydraulics, a live PTO and enough gears for most any job, yet it retains the low-slung compactness of the Ns. Diesel power was available in 1958.

Art Preston owns this 1959 Ford Model 981. With a 172 cubic inch, 47 horsepower engine, the 981 is an outgrowth of the 800 Series. It is designed to be convertible to a narrow front. It also has a two-speed (1000 rpm and 540 rpm) live PTO and a twelve-speed Selecto shift (shift-on-the-fly) transmission.

The 1958 Ford Model 501 Offset Workmaster from the Palmer Fossum Collection. The Workmaster was designed for single-row high-crop work, such as with sugar cane and grapes.

This 1958 Model 501 Offset Workmaster is part of the Fossum Collection. Designed for underbody-mounted tillage tools and an unobstructed view, the Offset is a departure from the Ford-Ferguson concept of rear-mounted implements, although the three-point hitch is retained. A substantial frame section is used, rather than relying on the engine structure to handle the loads.

The Workmaster used the 134 cubic inch Red Tiger engine of the Jubilee 600 Series, as well as the same four-speed transmission. This example also has a high-direct-low auxiliary transmission by Ford.

Two 12x38 rear tires help get the Work-master up above the crops. The front and back wheels are adjustable in width to accommodate row spacing.

Next page
This 1963 Fordson Triple-D (Doe Dual Drive), owned by Steve Lester of Pilton, England, was built at Maldon, Essex, England. It was a farmer's idea to join two Fordson Majors together to make one articulated four-wheel-drive tractor. The Triple-Ds were expensive, but they sold quite well, anyway. Many have been converted back to separate tractors since the availability of large four-wheel-drive tractors has increased.

Ford Tractors Today

Since tractors are not registered in the United States, it is difficult to say how many of the 820,207 Ford Tractors built are still in use. One Ford tractor dealer's service manager revealed that until 1985, he had never scrapped one out. In the years since 1985, he had found several that he considered to be beyond economical repair.

All parts, including sheet metal and trim items, are available from Ford tractor dealers and from several parts suppliers (see list of suppliers at the end of this book). Farm stores carry tune-up kits, batteries and other routinely replaced parts such as mufflers and tires.

Many handy individuals are now refurbishing Ford Tractors for resale, some doing as many as one per month. In 1990, a refurbished 8N brought about $2,500. One that had been restored, or brought back to new condition, would sell for about $5,000. The 9N and 2N models, being somewhat less desirable as work tractors, usually brought about 20 percent less. Interest by collectors is rapidly increasing, however, as is the value of older tractors, if they are in essentially original condition. Neither the 8N nor the 9N and 2N are so readily available that the buyer can expect to do much comparative shopping, though.

Advantages and disadvantages of Ford Tractors

The demand for the Ford Tractor is high because it is the most widely known used tractor of its size (20 to 30 horsepower) with the hydraulic three-point hitch. New or recent-vintage tractors of this size are all diesel powered. While this has a fuel-consumption advantage, it definitely adds to the price of the tractor. A comparable new tractor will sell for over $10,000.

As for performance and cost of operation, aside from fuel consumption, the Ford Tractor will do the same job as newer tractors. Harry Ferguson criticized Ford's archaic side-valve L-head engine, but in fact, Nebraska Tractor Tests rated the 8N as being better on fuel consumption than either the Ferguson TO-30 or the 8N's successor, the Ford Jubilee, both with modern overhead-valve engines.

One drawback to the Ford Tractor as compared with later tractors is the lack of live hydraulics and power takeoff. On the Ford Tractor, the hydraulic pump is driven by means of the PTO mechanism, and the PTO is driven only when the clutch is engaged. This means that implements cannot be raised when the clutch is depressed. For many applications, this is inconvenient. For example, the operator must put the transmission in neutral and release the clutch in order to raise a grader blade before backing. The next model, the 1953 Ford Jubilee, has live hydraulics.

A second drawback, compared with later tractors of this size, is the

The Fossum Collection also contains this 1952 Ford 8N with a Funk six-cylinder conversion. Everything said for the V-8 conversion goes for the 95 horsepower six, except that the exhaust is single. Much more common than the V-8, the Funk conversion to the Ford flathead six was used with irrigation pumps, silo fillers, threshing machines, pull-type combines and the Sherman backhoe. Conversion kits went for about $850 when introduced in 1949.

The Fossum Collection includes this 1952 Ford 8N with a Funk V-8 conversion. The Funk conversion consists of gearbox adapters and adapters for front wheel attachment. The tractor is lengthened, so tie and radius rods are extended, and a hood extension is provided to reach the instrument panel. The hood and grille are raised, and an appropriate radiator is used. Fossum has two vertical straight pipes for the exhaust—the sound is magnificent!

Palmer Fossum drives his 1952 Funk V-8 conversion—the Ford bull, if there ever was one! This is a rare conversion; most used industrial, or truck, sixes. Kits were offered by Funk Brothers of Coffeeville, Kansas, which also produced, in the forties, a light aircraft known as the Funk B. The added power was welcome for such chores as belt-powering threshing machines or for heavy mowing, where a good part of the power went through the PTO.

lack of a rollover bar. While most welding houses could fabricate one, the inconvenience and cost probably mean that most owners will take their chances. Sims Manufacturing of Rutland, Massachusetts, is now offering rollover bar kits for Ford and other tractors originally sold without.

For some, a third drawback is the 6 volt electrical system. Conversion to 12 volts is not difficult; the same 6 volt starter can be used. The 6 volt system is adequate, however, and there is really little reason to change.

When Ford and Ferguson got their heads together back in 1939, their brain child was primarily a plowing tractor, designed to do one acre per hour. Today, Ford Tractors are rarely used

The engine of Fossum's Funk V-8 conversion is an 8BA, 100 horsepower 1952 Ford powerplant. The man who sold this tractor to Fossum said, "Remember that you have a 100 horsepower engine and a 30 horsepower transmission and rear end, and you won't get in trouble."

To demonstrate the extent of new parts available to the rebuilder, Bill Ficken, manager of Strojney Implement of Mosinee, Wisconsin, holds a brand-new crankshaft for the N Series engines.

Also available from Strojney Implement is this brand-new hydraulic cylinder and control. The availability of such new parts greatly reduces the risk to the rebuilder.

The new N Series cylinder head is another example of new parts availability for the N Series Fords. Ficken maintains that it is possible to create a new serial number tractor from parts. Major castings are the problem, although they are not so complex that new molds could not be built, if someone were really determined.

for plowing fields. Most are used for mowing or loading, equipped with front-end loaders and separate engine-driven hydraulic pumps. Of the 400 plus implements designed for the three-point hitch and power takeoff, the most common are the grader blade, posthole auger, landscape scarifier, rotary mower, lifting boom, saw rig (for cutting firewood), box scraper (for moving earth) and drawbar (attached either to the three-point links or to the differential housing, for pulling trailers or other light implements). Without 300 plus pounds of calcium chloride liquid installed in the tires, Ford Tractors used in drawbar pulling cannot exert as much pull as a heavier tractor.

How to buy a Ford Tractor

After the first glimpse at the general condition of the tractor, there are

Here's how to buy a tractor

Just ask yourself: "Will this tractor do the most jobs for me, more of the time, without wasting power? Is it easy to operate, and will it go from one kind of a job to another, quickly and easily?"

To *answer* yourself, you've got to *see* the tractor do *your* jobs on your farm. And above all, you shouldn't let "habit" guide your choice.

This time, call your *Ferguson* Dealer. Ask him to prove the ability of the Ferguson "30" in a Showdown Demonstration on your farm. Let him show you how many bottoms it will pull in *your* soil. See how quickly and easily you, or anyone, can change implements with Ferguson's *time-proved* 3-point hookup. Then disc, or do any of the other jobs you'll be doing throughout the year.

You (and your family) will discover that the exclusive Ferguson System gives you a lot more tractor for a lot less money . . . a lot more farming, with a lot less work.

Call your Ferguson Dealer today. Set up a Showdown Demonstration on your farm *soon*. Chances are, you've already missed too much . . . too long!

FREE BOOKLET tells you "How to Buy a Tractor". 24 pages of valuable information! Your Ferguson Dealer has your copy, or write: Harry Ferguson, Inc., Detroit 32, Michigan. © 1953, H. F. INC.

Get your Showdown Demonstration of the Ferguson Manure Spreader and Loader. This exclusive Ferguson combination lets you load, hitch, haul and spread without leaving the tractor seat! Hydraulically operated, patented hook 'n' eye hitch lets you do this tough job alone, without drudgery.

No other tractor gives you *all* the Ferguson System advantages: Traction and penetration without power-stealing weight, finger tip and automatic draft control, front-end stability, and an exclusive built-in hydraulic overload release that saves tractor and implement if you hit a hidden rock or stump.

Seeing is Believing — Get Your Showdown Demonstration of the

FERGUSON "30"

Previous page
An ad for the new Ferguson tractor gives helpful advice on purchasing.

several things to look for immediately: Is it a 9N or 2N, or an 8N, and can you live with the brake pedal arrangement of the 9N or 2N? Is there a Sherman transmission? A 9N or 2N is especially handicapped without one, and although the Shifter can be added, it will be costly.

Next check the condition of the sheet metal, grille and fenders. Problems here do not affect performance but are relatively costly to rectify and, if not corrected, affect your contentment with the tractor. A new grille sells for about $60. Each hood side panel is about the same.

Now examine the hydraulics. The controls of these components are connected through 6 inch holes in the cast-iron housings, which requires considerable skill and dexterity. Two initial tests will reveal whether expensive repairs are required: First, the three-point hitch should raise a substantial load easily—it should lift 700 pounds at the uniball points. Second, once raised, the load should not settle or leak down for at least ten minutes. Good hitches will hold up a two-bottom plow overnight.

For some reason, the exhaust manifold is a weak point. The manifold side of the manifold/exhaust pipe interface will often crack off. A new manifold will cost $50 to $60. Installation is not difficult, but heat may be required to loosen the bolts.

Check for free movement of the steering wheel, measured at the rim with the front wheels straight ahead. No more than 4 inches of free play should be accepted as tolerable. Check for slack in the tie rod ends, kingpin looseness and front axle/radius rod looseness. Check for front wheel shimmy when operating in road gear at high speed.

This aftermarket accessory swirl-type air cleaner, shown on a Fossum Collection 1952 Ford 8N, was designed to centrifugally separate the big chunks out and into the glass bottle, while the rest proceeded through the standard oil bath air filter.

You should be able to lock either back wheel with its respective pedal on virtually any surface. The brakes are easily adjusted, if the adjusting mechanism has not seized from years of corrosion. Check scraping, metal-to-metal sounds that would indicate depletion of the brake lining. A grabby brake indicates the same thing. Weak brakes are usually caused by axle seal leakage.

The clutch should operate without requiring undue force; it should engage smoothly and there should be no slippage when it is fully engaged. There should be an inch or so of free play on the pedal. On the 9N or 2N, be sure the clutch pedal actuates the left brake sufficiently to slide the left tire. Also make sure the clutch releases completely, so that there is no raking of gears when moving the shift lever from neutral while standing still.

The original rear wheels were built up around the rim of a hat, or box-section, with bolts attaching the rim to each wheel disc. If calcium chloride was used and if the tire ever leaked, the fluid found its way into this semi-enclosed area and corrosion commenced. Most of these wheels have already been replaced, but if the ones on the tractor you're looking at have not been, count on doing so at around $75 each. As corrosion eats through, the sharp edges produced will cut the tube and you will be plagued by slow (and not-so-slow) leaks. Collectors,

who want their tractors original, will pay a premium for good-condition box-section rims.

Check the radiator for leaks, dirty fluid and inadequate cooling (due to blocked passages). For 9Ns, this is not a pressurized system, so there is no pressure cap to inspect. A new radiator is about $150, and old ones are difficult to repair. A note of caution on cooling: Be sure the fan belt is tight and in good condition. If the belt slips, engine heat will boil the fuel in the tank directly above. The Ford has a good vent system, but if for some reason it should be restricted, the fuel tank could rupture, spilling fuel onto the engine.

The tractor should start readily, hot or cold, although the choke will most likely be required for every start. If the tractor is reluctant to fire up, the starter may need overhauling and may be taking too much of the available power, leaving too little for adequate spark. In addition, original starter drives tended to kick out too early. A modified unit is available and is easily installed.

Look for a resistor in the circuit across the ammeter. Some owners have removed this in an effort to get more power to the coil for starting. If this resistor is not in place, however, point life will be quite short.

Once the tractor has been started, check the operation of the generator by noting an indication of charge on the ammeter. Pre 1948 tractors have no

voltage regulator, as such, only a cutout system.

It is possible to jump-start the 6 volt Ford Tractor to a 12 volt source, although the practice should be considered a last resort. Remember, the Ford has a positive-ground system, opposite to today's convention, so the cables will be reversed on one end. For best results, do not run the engine on the 12 volt source vehicle during the jump. This allows the voltage to drop some from the rated. Attach the red cable to the positive terminal and the black cable to the negative terminal on the source battery. Attach the red cable to a good unpainted ground point on the tractor (not the battery terminal). Then, with the key on and the transmission in neutral, touch the black cable to the tractor starter terminal. Pull the choke while the engine cranks. Limit cranking to ten to fifteen seconds, with five minutes' cooling between attempts.

With the engine running, listen for smooth operation and lack of knocking or valve clatter. Oil pressure should be 30 to 40 psi. If smoke comes from either the tailpipe or the oil filler breather, a compression check is in order. Compression should be 90 psi minimum. A compression check will also reveal whether an engine miss is caused by a burned valve or by an ignition problem. Factory-rebuilt engines are available for about $1,300 plus your old engine. Parts for a do-it-yourself overhaul will run about $450.

Specifications

Fordson serial numbers and specifications

Beginning numbers

Year	Dearborn	Cork
1917	1	
1918	260	
1919	34427	63001
1920	100001	65104

	Rouge	
1921	153812	108230
1922	201026	109673
1923	268583	
1924	370351	
1925	453360	
1926	557608	
1927		
1928		
1929		747682
1930		757369
1931		772565
1932		776066

		Dagenham
1933		779154
1934		781967
1935		785548
1936		794703
1937		807581
1938		826779
1939		837826
1940		854238
1941		874914
1942		897624
1943		925274
1944		957574
1945		975419
1946		993489

Horsepower	20 @ 1100 rpm
Engine	251 cubic inch 4 cylinder L-head
Powertrain	3 forward gears
Weight	2700 lb

Model 9N specifications

Wheelbase ...... 70 in.
Overall length .... 115 in.
Normal width .... 64 in.
Turning radius ... 8 ft.
Overall height .... 52 in.
Weight .... 2,340 lb
Front tire size 4x19
Rear tire size .... 8x32 early; 10x28 late
Front tread ...... 48–76 in.
Rear tread .... 52–76 in.

Notes: Wheelbase is reduced as front tread is increased. Normal width is calculated at minimum tread width. Weight is with gasoline, water and oil, but with no weight liquid in the tires.

Model 2N specifications

Wheelbase ...... 70 in.
Overall length .... 115 in.
Normal width .... 64 in.
Turning radius ... 8 ft.
Overall height .... 52 in.
Weight .... 2,340 lb
Front tire size 4x19
Rear tire size 10x28
Front tread ...... 48–76 in.
Rear tread .... 52–76 in.

Notes: Wheelbase is reduced as front tread is increased. Normal width is calculated at minimum tread width. Weight is with gasoline, water and oil, but with no weight liquid in the tires. For rear tires, 11.2x28 and 12x28 tires can also be used.

Model 8N specifications

Wheelbase ...... 70 in.
Overall length .... 115 in.
Normal width .... 64.75 in.
Turning radius ... 8 ft.
Overall height .... 54.5 in.
Weight .... 2,410 lb
Front tire size 4x19
Rear tire size 10x28
Front tread ...... 48–76 in.
Rear tread .... 48–76 in.

Notes: Wheelbase is reduced as front tread is increased. Normal width is calculated at minimum tread width. Weight is with gasoline, water and oil, but with no weight liquid in the tires. For rear tires, 11.2x28 and 12x28 tires can also be used.

Ford Tractors serial numbers

Model 9N

1939	1 to 10233
1940	10234 to 45975
1941	45976 to 88887
1942	88888 to 99002

Total production: 99,002

Model 2N

1942	99003 to 105374
1943	105375 to 126537
1944	126538 to 169981
1945	169982 to 198730
1946	198731 to 258503
1947	258504 to 296131

Total production: 197,129

Model 8N

1947	1 to 37907
1948	37908 to 141369
1949	141370 to 245636
1950	245637 to 343592
1951	343593 to 442034
1952	442035 to 524076

Total production: 524,076

Total 9N, 2N and 8N production: 820,207

Common N Series implements

Two-bottom plow
One-bottom plow
Disc
Spring tooth drag
Cultivator
Spike tooth drag
Sickle bar mower
Rotary mower
Saw rig
Hay rake
Grader blade
Front dozer, or snowplow
Box scraper
Posthole auger
Lifting boom
Scarifier
Rock rake
Flat-belt pulley

Ford Model NAA Golden Jubilee serial numbers and specifications
Beginning numbers
1953 .... NAA 1
1954 .... NAA 77475

Horsepower ...... 31 @ 2000 rpm
Engine .... 134 cubic inch
               4 cylinder
               overhead-valve
Powertrain .... 4 forward gears
Weight .... 2510 lb

TE-20 (imported) serial numbers
Beginning serial numbers
1948 20800
1949 77770

TO-20 (US built) serial numbers and specifications
Beginning serial numbers
1948 1
1949 1808
1950 14660
1951 39163

Horsepower ...... 22.53 @ 2000 rpm
Engine .... 120 cubic inch
               4 cylinder
               overhead-valve
               Continental
Powertrain .... 4 forward gears
Weight .... 2,550 lb

TO-30 serial numbers and specifications
Beginning serial numbers
1951 60001
1952 .... T072680
1953 .... T0108645
1954 .... T0125958

Horsepower ...... 29.32 @ 2000 rpm
Engine .... 129 cubic inch
               4 cylinder
               overhead-valve
               Continental
Powertrain .... 4 forward gears
Weight .... 2,840 lb

Sources

Central Tractor
3915 Delaware Ave.
Des Moines, IA 50316

Palmer Fossum
10201 E. 100th St.
Northfield, MN 55057

Goodman Tractor Supply
1200 East O St.
Lincoln, NE 68501

Strojney Implement Company
Mosinee, WI 54455

Tractor Supply Company
14242 C Circle Dr.
Omaha, NE 68144

Keith Oltrogge
Wild Harvest-Massey Collector News
171 East Main St.
Denver, IA 50622

Peder Bjerre
Varity Corporation
595 Bay St.
Toronto, Ontario M5G 2C3 Canada

Gerard Rinaldi
The 9N-2N-8N Newsletter
154 Blackwood Ln.
Stamford, CT 06903

Recommended Reading

Baldwin, Nick. *Farm Tractors*. London: Frederic Warne, 1977.

Fraser, Colin. *Tractor Pioneer*. Athens, Ohio: Ohio University Press, 1973.

Gray, R. B. *Development of the Agricultural Tractor in the United States*. St. Joseph, Michigan: American Society of Agricultural Engineers, 1956.

Larsen, Lester. *Farm Tractors 1950–1975*. St. Joseph, Michigan: American Society of Agricultural Engineers, 1975.

Williams, Michael. *Ford and Fordson Tractors*. Dorset: Blandford Press, 1985.

Index